T0129683

Fulfilling Your
DESTINY

Philip Arkoh & Jonathan Korley

WESTBOW
PRESS®
A DIVISION OF THOMAS NELSON
& ZONDERVAN

NKJV: Scripture quotations marked NKJV are taken from the New King James Version. Copyright 1982 by Thomas Nelson, Inc. Used by permission. All rights reserved.
NIV: Scripture quotations marked NIV are taken from the Holy Bible, New International Version. NIV. Copyright 1973, 1978, 1984 by International Bible Society. Used by permission of Zondervan. All rights reserved.
ISV: International Standard Version (New Testament). 2000. Yorba Linda, CA: The Learning Foundation.

This book is a work of non-fiction. Unless otherwise noted, the author and the publisher make no explicit guarantees as to the accuracy of the information contained in this book and in some cases, names of people and places have been altered to protect their privacy.

WestBow Press books may be ordered through booksellers or by contacting:

WestBow Press
A Division of Thomas Nelson & Zondervan
1663 Liberty Drive
Bloomington, IN 47403
www.westbowpress.com
1 (866) 928-1240

Because of the dynamic nature of the Internet, any web addresses or links contained in this book may have changed since publication and may no longer be valid. The views expressed in this work are solely those of the author and do not necessarily reflect the views of the publisher, and the publisher hereby disclaims any responsibility for them.

Any people depicted in stock imagery provided by Thinkstock are models, and such images are being used for illustrative purposes only. Certain stock imagery © Thinkstock.

ISBN: 978-1-9736-0354-2 (sc)
ISBN: 978-1-9736-0355-9 (hc)
ISBN: 978-1-9736-0353-5 (e)

Library of Congress Control Number: 2017915104

Print information available on the last page.

WestBow Press rev. date: 11/8/2017

Table of Contents

Introduction

God did not make human race for pleasure or for fun. Man, might have been created out of love and delight, yet he is never in any way a creative toy meant for His enjoyment. God made man for a purpose just as He made all things. Every created being expresses the Creator's idea or solution. Man, was made as a solution to an existing problem. That is what the Bible says. The verse five of Genesis 2 says, "*…and there was not a man to till the ground.*" That was why Adam was made according to the Bible. All creatures were made to solve existing problems, and the problem you solve defines who you are.

When you hear about the Sun, right away an idea comes into mind. You know what it is by the purpose it serves. This is same with you and me. We are here to solve problems, and the problem you solve is your destiny. The pages of history are filled with this; men who for all they could have done lived their lives to solve problems. Most of the things we enjoy today are solutions to problems that once existed. This world has been blessed with men and women who throughout all their lives lived solving existing problems in any field of endeavor these fields ranged from the sciences, medicine, engineering, politics, entrepreneurship, banking and finance, architecture, to technology. We heard as children how life was like, back in the 20th century; how men could walk great distances just to purchase little items.

I remember being told by my grandfather how he could walk for over hundred miles just to purchase salt and walk the same distance back home. There were times that men walked barefooted and lived in caves in most part of the world. I heard that people could walk hundreds of miles just to relay information to other people in different towns. But interestingly all these have changed in today's world thanks to men and women who gave themselves to making this happen. Every individual has something to offer. Please understand that you are not just here to take from this world but contribute to this world. This world is waiting to hear from you. You have lots to deliver.

If we were all made to solve problems just as destiny is defined here, then I bet you; this world would have been a better place if we were to live to make it so by responding to our individual destinies. Remember that your destiny is the problem you solve here. Discover this and live for it until the world can feel you. Be an asset to this world and not a liability. The problem with the world today is the fact that there are too many liabilities than assets. There are too many people depending on the world than people the world is depending on. And when the situation remains like this, the world will keep suffering.

There are people with great ideas and inventions hidden deep within them the world is not benefiting. I believe there are people with solutions scattered all around we need to know. And you, my reader, is one of them. The world needs you to be able to survive. Ignore those who think you are useless or ordinary and start doing what you need to do to make your world a better place. The only useless person I know is the one who has chosen to live a meaningless life. Stop wandering from one thing to the other and make a discovery of yourself and pursue it. There is something God made you to be or do, which would be a great blessing to mankind should you pursue it. This is what you need to consider if you want to be influential. Stop imitating people and be your original self.

I know some people like to copy or imitate what others are doing which is not a bad idea. But understand that if you are like that you don't go as far as you can go in life. Just as there are no two people with the same fingerprint in this world, there are no two-same people. No matter how an identical twin may resemble each other they are not the same, and can never have an identical fingerprint. There is something peculiar you have in you, which defines who and what you are.

Before you came into this world, heaven had already decided your destiny. Just as Joseph was intended a prime minister in Egypt to solve a problem, David was heaven's intended King in his time. Like these men, God has an already planned life for you no matter your race, tribe or tongue. It is a life of honor, glory and greatness. You might have begun small and little, but let the end define you instead of the beginning. The book of Job 8:7 clearly shows that one's beginning does not define him but his end. It says, ***"though thy beginning was small, yet thy latter end should greatly increase***." How you begin something is not as important as the end. You were never intended by God to be ordinary. The Bible says you are the light of the world, and this means that you were made for influence and impact. You were made to be a world changer, miracle worker and a performer of mighty deeds. You were made to be an up lifter of souls, a champion and a hero. You are never in God's plan as a victim or loser.

Every individual is a potential winner or victor in this life. My advice to you is not to despise any individual in this life, for everyone is a potential success. Don't judge their lives looking at their present situations. It will interest you to know that some of the people you underrate are destined world changers, scientists, doctors, preachers and impact makers. The Bible says that, had the leaders of the Jews and of the world known that the man that they were persecuting and killing was actually their long-awaited messiah, they wouldn't have done that. Rise and make a discovery of yourself, then go out there and win. You are a mighty man or woman.

Have you read what the angel of the Lord told Gideon at first sight? He called him, "A mighty man of valor." That was interesting seeing that Gideon, the man who the angel was referring to didn't see himself as such. He called himself poor and least. This is one of the greatest things that can happen to a man, and that is to make a discovery of who you really are. Stop seeing yourself as others view you and begin to see yourself as God sees you. Your family might not have planned for your coming but God did. You might have been branded an unwanted child, yet God's idea about you hasn't changed. You are still the problem solver He made. Do you know that at the time that Moses was born, his parents were not expecting a boy, owing to the fact that at the time every male child born to any Jew was executed? I believe his parents were expecting a girl instead, yet it is not always as men wish. The counsel and plan of God always prevailed.

My dear, God knew you before you were formed, and He designed what you should become even before you came out of the womb. Heaven has a record of you and there are angels who report back to God concerning your life. You are a man of honor, so rise up and become what you were made to be. You are God's given answer and solution, so do not fret. Just respond to destiny's call. The world is waiting for your manifestation, man of influence. I am speaking to you who is reading this book. You are not ordinary.

Forget your past and forge on. It is not about where or what you have been, but what you can become. Discover who you are and where you fit in life and pursue it. Become what God wants you to be and you will be a great blessing to your nation and the world in general. Stop calling yourself worthless when the Lord says that you are worthy. Why do you brand yourself a non-entity when the Lord says you are important? God does not make anything unimportant. Everything He made, He said it was good. You can be very useful. All you have got to do is to make a discovery of yourself. Know who you are and what you stand for, and you will be on your way to achieving great feat in this life. The fulfillment of your destiny is one of the most beautiful things that can happen to you.

Five Facts About Your Destiny

1. Your destiny was decided even before you were born

Destiny is God ordained, and not man ordained. This means what you are to become in this life is God's decision. It is neither yours nor your family's decision. And God decides your destiny before birth, not after birth. In Jeremiah 1: 5, the Lord made Jeremiah aware of this truth.

"Before I formed thee in the belly I knew thee; and before thou camest forth out of the womb I sanctified thee, and ordained thee a prophet unto the nations." Jeremiah 1:5

This world was planned and created by God, and He is the One who assigns roles. And it is He who knows where you fit. He knows what you are good at as well as what you are bad at. He knows your gifting, abilities and potentials as well as your weakness. You are His creation and hand work. And he knows the role you can play in a world He created. Just understand that before everything else began, God had you in mind, and He brought you here to fulfil a particular course.

In Galatians 1: 15, the Apostle Paul again stresses on this important fact: Destiny is decided before you were born. It says, *"…when it pleased God who separated from my mother's womb, and called me by his grace"* Galatians 1:15

Have it in mind from today that who you are, has been decided by God already, and that, no one can change what He made you to become. And again, be reminded that whatever He made you to be, is the greatest thing that you can ever be in life. Your destiny is decided before you arrive into this world.

2. Your destiny is already documented and sealed

A friend once told me of a dream he had where he saw a very big book shown him by an Angel of the Lord. He said, in the book, there were written names and assignments attached to each of the names. Right there I told him I believe what he was saying, because of what is written in Hebrews 10:7. It says, *then said I, Lo, I come (in the volume of the book it is written of me,) to do thy will, O God.*

Heaven has a documentation of what every individual should become. I believe that there is a book that has your name and assignment. I know my mission here on earth was documented and sealed in heaven before I was even born. So is yours. Don't be a victim of circumstance. Never allow your situation to dictate what you should become. Become what heaven wants you to be and you shall blossom. God will not change what you should become, because you don't want it or you desire something else. As the purpose for the sun, moon and the other creation of God is sealed, so is your purpose sealed. If you will shine, it is in what you were made to be. Your brightness and glory in this life is dependent on becoming what you were made to be. So, get up and shine!

3. Your destiny is your personal discovery

One of the reasons why most individuals do not become who they were made to be or fulfil their God ordained destinies is their inability to make a discovery of who they are. Self discovery is very key in self manifestation. You can't manifest your full potential until you know who you are and what you have. One day a hunter brought a baby lion home from hunting, and when he came he added that young cub to his flock of sheep. But instead of that cub growing to become like a lion, it grew up having the body and appearance of a lion but with a different behavior. It grew up acting and behaving like one of those sheep it grew up with. But one day, the whole flock was attacked by a lion just like this lion when they were taken to graze, and on seeing this lion just like itself roar and act courageously chasing those sheep around trying to tear them up until their owner showed up to drive that lion away, it realized that there was more to itself it didn't know, so it followed the other lion into the jungle.

This story indicates how important self discovery is in the life of every individual. In order to fully manifest yourself, you need to know who you are. And searching out to obtain that self knowledge about who you are is yours to do and not God's. God decides your destiny but understand that its discovery is your repsonsibiltiy. Though most times God helps us to identify when we seek, but it lies on us to discover. Do not waste time again. Get up, seek and identify who you are so that you can fully manifest yourself in this world. Discover who you are, what you have and what you can do and become a blessing to your generation. Remember that others may help you to discover yourself but self discovery is mainly yours to do so don't wait for anyone. Discover yourself so you can live the life God wants you to live on earth.

4. Your destiny cannot be altered, you just refuse to become it and by so doing become something else

Your destiny is your assignment in this life or the role you play in God's world. And all the abilities He gave you was because of who He made you to be. Yet understand that though your destiny is decided by God, fulfilling it is your choice and decision. God decides who you are, but what you become is your choice. Understand that God does not change who He made you to be. In other words, God does not change destiny, instead we choose to become something else. Remember that every individual enjoys his very best in life when he or she is fulfilling purpose. You will be easily seen when you are fulfilling destiny. Fulfilling your destiny is the best way to impact your world. You easily rise to glory when the fulfilment of your destiny is your priority. Do not be lured or enticed to become who you are not. Be yourself and press to make what you stand for happen, and the world will her about you.

One more thing you need to know is that you are easily seen when fulfilling destiny. The sun is best seen when shining. Remember that your destiny is the reason why you possess the gifts and abilities you have. Have you asked yourself why some people can sing with ease but others cannot and why others run very well and with ease but others cannot. You can do what you do with ease because you were made to. You are the only one who can be what you are meant to be, that is why you were given such gifts and talents. You may refuse to be what God wants you to be but His purpose for your life remains and will not be changed. God will not change the purpose of birds, because a bird chose not to fly. Your purpose is yours to fulfill.

5. No one, including the devil can stop you from fulfilling your destiny, except yourself

The fulfillment of your destiny is your decision. God will never force you into it but will let you know and understand why you have to become it. And again no one can stop you from becoming what you need to be. The only one who can stand between you and your destiny is you. No one has the power to stop you from becoming what you were made to be. After Jesus died and rose for you, you became unstoppable. He conquered the devil for you so that you could get through to your destined end. You must not allow anything to stop you from getting to your destination, after all that Jesus did for you. The awesome thing now is that He is in you as a strength urging you on to extra ordinary heights. Greater is He that is in you than he that is in this world (1 John 4:4). Fear not, you can achieve anything now. You can do the impossible and the uncommon. Anything is possible to the man who believes. Let nothing cease you from becoming what you should be. The most powerful force in the world is for you and not against you. Get up and walk in this reality so that you can achieve the uncommon.

If all you dream for is to be able to fulfill your God given destiny and to become what God wants you to be, then this book is designed for you. It will show you what you need in order to be where God wants you to be. It is also a boost for those who are already on their way to fulfillment. Never forget this that God longs to see you on top than you even desire to rise. He has the best in store for you and He is ever ready and willing to take you there. This book, is an exposé' on the life of David and will show you what you need to ascend that throne of destiny. It unveils the six simple but great secrets that made David the King God intended. And it will make you too. The lessons outlined here are proven and will not fail anyone who applies or run with them. These are lessons that are clearly shown by the lives of all the history makers the Bible records and even in the history of our world at large. The scripture below shows these six secrets that will make you:

Then answered one of the servants, and said, Behold, I have seen a son of Jesse the Bethlehemite, [that is] **cunning in playing**, *and a* **mighty valiant man**, *and* **a man of war**, *and* **prudent in matters**, *and a* **comely person**, *and* **the LORD [is] with him.** 1 Samuel 16:18

Stay blessed as you keep reading, and may you receive any blessing you need to achieve success and breakthrough.

Chapter 1

DISCOVER YOUR GIFTS AND ABILITIES

> Then answered one of the servants, and said, Behold, I have seen a son of Jesse the Bethlehemite, **[that is]** CUNNING IN PLAYING and a mighty valiant man, and a man of war, and prudent in matters, and a comely person, and the LORD is with him. (1 Samuel 16:18)

No one was created without a gift or an ability. Everyone has a gift. Every individual is potent at something. There is something you can do well that others may do, but they don't do it like you do it. Every person is in a way different from others. You are different from me. We may look alike but are not the same. Your gift distinguishes you. A dog barks while a cat meows. A horse runs while a tortoise crawls. Yet they are all animals. What you are gifted at gives you easy identification. I know that when you hear a dog barking, no one tells you it is a dog even when it is not in sight. Your gift makes you unique. This is the first truth you need to know and understand if you want to rise to any enviable position. Joseph needed his ability to interpret dreams on his way to becoming a prime minister as much as David needed his harp playing and music ability on his way to becoming a king. Daniel's ability to interpret dreams and hard sayings opened a door for him even in slavery. God works through our gifts to achieve His purposes. In order to get to your destined grounds, a gift is very important. Your gifts are like the farming tools in the hands of a farmer, or the medical equipment in the hands of a doctor. You cannot execute your mission without the role that a gift plays. The gift you possess has an important link to your destiny. A person's gifts are the tools needed to get the person going till he or she gets to the destination.

Though David was anointed to be king over Israel, he was still living in the wilderness. The Lord had spoken to the prophet Samuel, who was then His mouthpiece to anoint David, and he did. But David was still shut in the wilderness. You see, to be anointed is not to be enthroned. The anointing on a person's life brings approval and comes to help him or her through the process of ascending the throne.

David stayed in the wilderness until he was spotted using his gift. "Behold I have seen a son of Jesse, who is a cunning player" (1 Samuel 16:18). In other words, Saul's servant spotted one of the sons of Jesse skillfully using his gift. And this was the beginning of his breakthrough. His gift had given him access. This was at a time that the king was tormented by evil spirits and was in dire need of a musician who was master in his field. And David was chosen. Never forget that before this, he was already anointed to be king in the stead of Saul. But David never had the opportunity to come close to the palace, which was spiritually his until his gift gave him that introduction. Your gift will make way for you where you have no link. You will be seen when using your gift. Your gift will determine your lift.

Six Things Your Gift Will Do for You

1. Your gift will give you the access you are looking for.

It was David's gift that gave him access to the palace, which was spiritually his. Joseph's gift brought him before Pharaoh. It was also

Joseph's gift that paved the way for him to meet Pharaoh. Similarly, it is your gift that will give you the access you need to your destiny. Your gift will give you entry to the Promised Land.

2. You will not attract the attention of those who will be your helpers and promoters until they see your gift.

It was not Joseph's words that linked him—it was his gift. The chief butler had noticed the gift he possessed, and then the butler remembered him for that. Do you remember what that servant of Saul who connected David said? "I have seen the son of Jesse the Bethlehemite that is a cunning player" (1 Samuel 16:18). I believe this man might have heard David singing and playing the harp somewhere and had fallen in love with his gift and skill. There are always people who are there to promote our destinies, and we only meet these people when our gifts are in use. All you need to do is develop and use your gift, and then you will be noticed. When your gift is in operation, it will be to your own advantage. You need to be discovered by those who are meant to be your destiny helpers, and it is your gift that will bring you that discovery.

3. Your gift will position you to view your destiny in clarity.

The throne Saul sat on was not David's inheritance—it was his destiny. The Lord gave him that throne and was going to establish him on it forever, but he never came any closer until his gift positioned him so close to it. Only God knows what went through David's mind anytime he sat beside that throne, playing and singing for King Saul. I believe it gave him the opportunity to envision himself seated on that throne. This fulfils that law that says, "You become what you see." Until you can see it, you cannot become it. The extent of your vision is your limitation. He or she who sees the invisible will do the impossible. I believe David always saw himself seated on that throne, reigning over Israel.

4. Your gift is your key.

A gift is what you need to unlock any door. I often tell people that God does not open doors; He rather gives us the key to open the doors. Look through the pages of scripture and you will see this. Jesus told Peter that He was going to give him the keys to the kingdom. And I believe these keys were meant to be used to open the doors of the kingdom. "I will give you the keys" is God's message. To access any door in this life, we need the right keys. And God always gives the key you need to access any door. And one of those keys is the gift you possess. Your gift opens the door to your destiny. Everyone has a gift, whether he or she knows it or not. And just as God used the rod in Moses's hand to open the Red Sea, He will always use your gift to open destiny's door. This is the reason why the discovery, development, and mastery of our gifts is very important in life. Your gift is the key to unlocking what the future has in store for you and humanity. That gift in your possession will pave the way for you like Moses's rod opened the Red Sea. God has given you the gift you possess as the key to unlocking the door to your destiny. He will give you the key you require to open that door. Jesus told Peter that he has been given the keys to the kingdom. A key will help you access your room of blessing. Most people have gotten nowhere near their destinies because the gift that will connect them to that place is undeveloped.

5. Your gift will create the right atmosphere for you to operate.

"A man's gift maketh room for him" (Proverbs 18:16).

No person is effective in the wrong atmosphere. No matter how powerful you are, without a good atmosphere you will struggle. And your gift can help you build the right atmosphere for success. And an example of a good atmosphere is in the midst of people who accept and celebrate who you are. Jesus flourished in Capernaum but struggled in Nazareth, His own hometown, due to atmosphere. You become your very best where you are accepted.

6. Your gift will give you a seat among champions.

There is a proverb in my country that says, "The child who knows how to wash his or her hand eats with the elderly." Most times in life, we see an introduction of an upcoming individual amongst the list of the great. And for any person you see following or among the great in his or her field of endeavor, it was this person's gift that brought that favor. It is always an honor to be found seated or positioned among honorable people. The first time I had the opportunity to sit among some people of honor in God's kingdom, all I could think about was this one truth. Your gift will create a seat for you among great individuals.

Develop Your Gift and Use It

As much as a gift is important in ascending any throne, an undeveloped gift amounts to nothing. It is not enough to have a gift—you must develop it. This is the difference between those who climb higher using their gifts and those who do not despite the numerous gifts they have. An undeveloped gift will take you nowhere. I don't think David was an amateur when his ability was noticed. I believe he was skilled in the art of music. The English Standard Version puts it this way: "Behold I have seen the son of Jesse who is a skillful player" (1 Samuel 16:18). If you really want to go far with your gift, add skill to it. Train yourself till you shine in it. Take what you have and polish it. If you sing, add value to yourself. Whatever you do, improve in it until you become the best. The world only chases and celebrates developed gifts. If they see that you are outstanding in what you do, you will become valuable to them. People will pay money to hear you speak because your words are inspiring and life changing. Give yourself to constant and continuous training till you begin to produce quality in what you do. One day I had a complaint from a group of singers in a respectable organization about their leaders going in for singers from other places during big events while they are there. You see, sometimes it is good to use what you have, but the truth is that, everyone likes quality. The one who is an expert in what he or she does, go far. Have you ever wondered about why you are as gifted as those on top yet it seems no one has taken notice of you? This is because your gift is untrained. Sharpen your gift and it will have easy penetration. Abraham Lincoln said "if I have eight hours to cut down a tree, I will use six hours to sharpen my axe, and use the remaining two hours to cut the tree." In other words, he would spend time developing his gift and then goes out to use it.

All those who become amazing in their respective fields, spend great time developing their gifts, abilities and also attitudes, after which they then come out to showcase what they have. This is what most people have missed. They go out chasing fame and success and then become disappointed when they do not get it. Improve your gift and it will fetch you great returns. Develop what you have until you become better at it and success will follow you. Do what you know to do well and you will see the rewards that will come to you. It is not enough to know that you have a gift, add value to it. The rewards from a developed gift are far greater than an undeveloped gift. Do you know why some gifted men are in high demand? It is because they are exceptional in what they do. This explains why some footballers are more valuable than others. No wonder some team owners do not care paying millions of pounds or dollars to have them in their teams. Any well-developed gift is valuable and expensive. It is not enough to be a singer, teacher, preacher, doctor, lawyer, sportsman and the other wonderful gifts you know. Add value to yourself by developing what you have and it will take you far. Be an expert when it comes to the use of your gifts and abilities. Sharpen what you do until you see yourself riding in excellence. Just forget about success and then chase excellence and you will see that success will follow you everywhere. Improve yourself and become best at what you do, and then you will see the rewards that will come to you.

Six Ways to Develop Your Gift

1. ***Set a goal for yourself and invest quality time and effort to achieving it.***

This is an important thing to consider before anything else begins. Make a decision on who you want to become or what you want to become. If you do not know what you want to be become, you might end up becoming just anything in life. First of all, set a target for yourself and then make the move to achieve it. Decide to become the best of what you can be and pursue it. For example, if you are a musician, who do you want to minister like or how do you want to minister?. Get all these questions answered before you set off because it will help you map out a clear route to realize your goal. After that, strive to become the best in your respective field. Let becoming the best, be your only option.

> *Good, Better, Best*
> *May I never rest!*
> *Until my Good be better!*
> *And my better Best*

This is a poem I remember singing back in Kindergarten days. It never made any meaning to me then until few years ago. I then told myself to never rest until I become the best of me. It became a good motivating poem for me as I pursued my dream of evangelism or any time I purpose to do anything. What I want is the best. What of you? How good do you dream to be? Set a target for yourself and stretch yourself to be it. If you sing, teach, play the piano or whatever your gift is, set a target for yourself and push until you get there.

Don't just be good; keep pushing until you become the best. Becoming the best in your field of endeavor requires a great deal of effort and energy, so invest your best shots and you will get to see the best of yourself.

2. Use your gift always.

You cannot develop something you do not use. You learn how to sing by singing. I didn't become a good teacher of the Word of God in a day, it is continuous preaching and teaching of the Word of God that has shaped my message. Keep using your gift till you don't find it difficult using it. Just a day driving will not make you an experienced driver. The more you use your gift, the easier and experienced you will be at using it it. It is the continuous usage of your gift that will make you a master at it. I once witnessed a young man playing classical music, and when asked about how he is able to play those keys on his piano with ease and skill, he smiled and said it took him over a decade of constant rehearsing and playing. No athlete becomes the best by just a day's practice. They keep doing that one thing all the time until they become best at it. I once read an article about a footballer who became a specialist in taking free kicks by constant rehearsals each day. Be dedicated to using your gift for the least opportunity you get.

3. Discipline yourself to do this every day and continuously.

Another thing which is needful for you to do is to be able to restrain yourself from going after anything which can take your attention off your dream so that you can keep working at your dream goal until you realize it. Discipline is prerequisite if you will be able to achieve any desired result in this life. Learn to control yourself to follow all routines so that you can be the best. Keep practicing and rehearsing. Do not stop if you don't get any better results at the initial stages of your practice. Keep improving yourself by investing effort.

4. Decide to become better each time until you can use your gift with ease.

Seek improvement in your performances anytime you get the opportunity to use your gift. Always work on yourself so as to get better results anytime you use your gift. If you get good performance today make sure the next one become excellent. Make this decision so that you don't program yourself to relax after every performance but then you put yourself to work any time. Fortunately for me I have friends who always remind me of what lays ahead to be accomplished after any achievement. There is always more you can do or achieve. You can be the very best of yourself. For me, anything I am able to accomplish is not always enough. I never arrive. This is why I keep pressing on like Paul to get to the mark of my high calling in Christ Jesus. Keep pushing too. Do not stop at being just a good person in your field. You can also be the best so strive for that.

5. *You can also learn from those who have similar gifts and are far ahead.*

For everything you want or want to achieve, remember there is someone who has what you want or has achieved what you aspire to achieve. There are people who have been successful in your chosen field of endeavor before. And the easiest way to become successful is to learn from those who have been ahead of you. This can save you years of wandering and life threatening mistakes. Be a follower of some of their good examples and also learn to avoid the mistakes they made.

Again, associate yourself with people who can add to your gift or help you to improve. Sharpen yourself with other irons like yourself, for iron sharpeneth iron. Get close to those who have similar gifts and are excelling. Learn new skills or ways of using your gift from those who are excelling and add them to what you already know.

6. *Be determined not to give up until you get the results you are looking for.*

Determined efforts in any given area of endeavor always pay off When we do not give up. One thing you need to understand is that there will always be times you might feel like giving up and doing something else. Please don't! It is a normal feeling on the way to achievement. I have felt like quitting several times in my life. But then I do not follow what I feel. For me that feeling is even a great announcement that I am so close to achieving my dream. I understand the frustrations and disappointments in failing on several counts when you try to develop your gift. Yet do not give up in those times when things are not working the way you want it to be.

There will be instances or seasons that will make everything look like you can never be as skillful as you want and that you are wasting your time. The difference between those who become successful in the use of their gifts and those who do not is their ability to ignore that feeling of defeat and refusing to quit, but instead press on till they realize their dream. Quitters never win and winners never quit. Keep trying and the results you are looking for will definitely happen. Do you know that I nearly gave up on writing this manuscript? But here you are reading it. Right now, giving up on anything is no more an option in life. *It is said that no man can dismantle the flag of success wherever determination is.* Keep on pressing till you get to your intended dream. What you desire is possible if you won't give up. Be determined to be the finest or the best in your field of endeavor and great returns will come to you.

Chapter 2

DEVELOP A COURAGEOUS ATTITUDE

*... and a **MIGHTY VALIANT MAN** ...* 1Samuel 16:18

This is one of the character traits that distinguished David, and it will also distinguish anyone who has it. To be valiant is to be brave or courageous. A brave or courageous attitude is very important if any man can get to his promised land. Courage is the quality of mind or spirit that enables a person to face difficulty, danger, pain and trouble without retreating or giving up. On the highway to fulfillment, there always come problems which may appear to scare you off. Oppositions of dreams and aspirations usually arise that always frighten people and make them retreat, but a truly courageous man will persist. Emerson once said;

"Whatever you do, you need courage. Whatever course you decide upon, there is always someone to tell you that you are wrong. There are always difficulties arising that tempt you to believe your critics are right. To map out a course of action and follow it to an end requires some of the same courage that a soldier needs. Peace has its victories, but it takes brave men and women to win them."

B. C. Forbes also stated, *"History has demonstrated that the most notable winners usually encountered heartbreaking obstacles before they triumphed. They won because they refused to become discouraged by their defeats."*

Every success story has in it a moment that required great measure of courageous efforts to get things done. Almost all successful men have always come to the point where they nearly threw down the towel but forged on in courage refusing to give up. Joseph's dreams spoke for themselves that he had a great destiny. He was going to rise above all his brethren and become one of the greatest men who ever rose in his time. Despite the fact that this was meant to be, the events which happened after his numerous dreams could have shuttered this dream or altered his course had he given in. He refused to give up but through courage and the help of God he defied the odds and rose to the very top. Every man or woman needs courage to survive. It is still the survival of the fittest. The fearful easily perishes. Anything defeats the fearful person but those of true courage win.

Great men like Nelson Mandela have always been men of courage and of great act of bravery. By their act of courage, they were able to do the impossible. This has been the difference between those who get on in life and those who do not; their act of bravery. The Bible is a book dedicated to telling the stories of brave men and women who stood for a particular cause. The testimony on the lives of those men and women of faith recorded in Hebrews 11 is what I call "the bravery roll call". Brave men stopped the mouth of lions. Brave men took over new lands. Brave men won wars. Bravery always achieved in the Bible days and it is still achieving contemporary results. Do you know that the discoveries, inventions, change and advancement this world is enjoying are products of bravery and courage? Science and medicine have greatly improved due to the fact that some people were brave and courageous. It was the act of courage that took men to the moon. When Neil Armstrong made his famous statement, "That's one small step for man, one giant leap for mankind" when he first stepped on the moon, it was the voice of bravery speaking.

Courage will take whoever has it a step forward. It will take you to where you have not been in life before. Courage is the gateway to the impossible, unthinkable, uncommon and unimaginable. It takes courage to believe and do something different when everyone believes the contrary. Do you know that it is only an act of courage that will take a gifted man to a new level and height? Andre Gide said, *"Man cannot discover new oceans unless he has the courage to lose sight of the shore."* All explorers are men of courage. It was the courageous act of Columbus that led to the discovery of ancient America. It takes courage to summon new things. Harry S. Truman also said, *"Men make history and not the other way around. In periods where there is no leadership, society stands still. Progress occurs when courageous, skillful leaders seize the opportunity to change things for the better."* If I were you, I would stop asking God for progress but will pray like the Apostles prayed. In Act 4:29, they asked that God would strengthen them to act and live in all boldness and courage so that they continue the work which they were made to do. This is because courage engineers progress. Courage answers the reasons why many change seekers do not get the change they want. The two door posts to the promised land are to be strong and be of good courage (Joshua 1:6). The promised land is not for weaklings; it belongs to brave people. Sometime ago I took time to ponder on why, some of the people of Israel had lands and had bigger portions whereas others got smaller portions. I didn't understand why the land was promised to all of them, yet some prospered than others. I also didn't understand the fact that some became poor while others excelled and became rich. Then I discovered that courage was the difference between them. Each tribe had to step out in courage and bravery to possess their possession, so was every individual. I realized that the promise land was a reward to courageous men, not fearful men. The actual bread is given to courageous men, but the portion of the fearful shall be the left over. Read the story of Joshua and Caleb in the book of **Numbers 13:30, 14:6-38** and you will see the rewards of courage. I was not surprised at all when I read in **Joshua 15: 16** that Caleb chose to give his daughter to a man of courage.

I remember before we started getting our expected results in our outreaching, the Lord told me to decide on what I want and then be brave to go for it. I then sat down and thought about the kind of results I had always anticipated, and then mustered the courage to go for it. Since then every new level I had gotten to was achieved by courage. Daring to achieve something new is like sailing unknown ocean, it takes great courage. This is because it is risky and adventuorous. All great achievements in my life are products of great acts of courage, whereas all defeats I have encountered are results of acts of fear. Fear cripples results where courage produces it. No matter how anointed you are, if you dwell in fear, you can never achieve much in life. God does not pamper fear. Scripture shows that all the individuals He used were daring men. God might have spoken to you to do something, yet you need to be courageous to get that task done. You can lose what God intends to give you because of fear. This is what happened to the Israelites who were not allowed to enter the promise Land. All God wanted them to do was to muster courage and forge on, and everything would have been theirs. But instead they gave in to fear and murmured and lambasted the Lord greatly, and as a result they were hindered. Never think that because God has said it, you don't have to make any move. A courageous move from you is what will get you to your destination. If you know any man of honor in your nation, state or region, visit them and ask how they got to where they are, and I tell you that none of them will exclude an act of courage because every man of honor has a report on courage hidden at the back of their success story. Heroes and heroines are all products of courage.

God has a lot of wonderful things in stock for everyone, but it is courage that will take you there. Fear has done nothing good to humanity. It has never taken anybody far. The achievements of fear have only been that of failure, poverty and death. Look through the pages of the Bible and you will see that, it is full of reports on what bravery and courage achieved. God is a rewarder of courage and responds to courage.

Come Boldly

Do you even know that God does not want us before His throne in fear and timidity? We are admonished to come boldly and not fearfully before the throne of grace.

Hebrews 4: 16 says, ***"Let us come boldly unto the throne of grace, that we may obtain mercy, and find grace to help in times of need"***

In other words, courage is key in accessing what grace has made available. This indicates that no matter what God has placed or prepared for you, if you approach Him in fear, you can't receive anything. I am made to believe especially by the scripture above that some people approach His throne in fear, trembling and full of doubt wondering whether they deserve anything good from Him. Others too come full of guilt from past mistakes and sins. You need to understand that God already knows you in that present state, yet His invitation is for you to come boldly to His throne of grace. Please, pause for a second and check the name given to God's throne. He didn't just call His seat, "Throne" but *"Throne of Grace"*. Grace is God's unmerited favor, which is, getting from God what you don't deserve. Hallelujah! Is this not interesting? God knows that you looked unworthy, yet He says where He sits is the throne of getting what you don't deserve, and when you come, you won't get what you deserve (death and condemnation). So, come, but don't just come, instead come courageously and obtain. This is the call from the throne of grace. God does not want you in His presence in fear and panic. Be bold and courageous, fear not for He is with you. He reminds us that we don't have the spirit of fear, but of boldness. Dare to believe Him and you won't be disappointed.

It is not enough to be just gifted. Any gift demonstrated through courage releases power. Henry Van Dyke said, ***"Genius is talent set on fire by courage."*** Minister with courage and you will produce amazing results. David was not just an ordinary gifted man; he was also a mighty valiant man. He was very brave, and this was one of the main things behind his success. Since fearful men achieve nothing, I believe David exhibited a courageous lifestyle. That was how I think the servant of King Saul got to know him, because at the time, David was not part of the army and couldn't have been just imagined as brave. Look at his testimony on how he handled the lion and the bear, and you will notice that he was actually bold in real life. The story of success or greatness throughout history has always been born on the grounds of bravery or adventure. This has always been the place where life separates men of honor from mean men. You cannot ply the road of destiny without courage. Abdul Kalam had this message to the youth of his day; "***My message, especially to young people is to have courage to think differently, courage to invent, to travel the unexplored path, courage to discover the impossible and to conquer the problems and succeed. These are great qualities that they must work towards. This is my message to the young people***". And I repeat this today to the young men of our world, without courage nothing will be achieved. Let us rise in strength and boldness, approaching issues in great courage and most of the problems in our days will be solved.

This is why the Lord had to tell the Israelites in Joshua 1:6, to be bold and courageous. Your destiny is yours for the taking but courage will take you there.

Step Out in Boldness

Do you know that it is one thing to have a gift, talent or ability, and another to blossom in that gift? It is one thing to have an idea and another to implement that idea. See how many a man had great ideas to do great things, but these ideas were never born, instead they died out while in the womb of thought. I am one of those who believe that there are lots of great inventions and discoveries the world should have enjoyed which were never born. Lots of companies and businesses, books, movies, speeches, music and other world changing organizations which could have been out by now but are still in the womb of thought as just mere ideas. An idea is powerless or useless until it is expressed or implemented, and it takes courage to implement an idea. It also takes great amount of courage to step out into the unknown. Ideas are important. We must have ideas to create and improve anything. Success avoids the man who lacks ideas. An idealess man is a worthless man. Everyone needs ideas to break forth. But it is sad to know, that thousands of people bury good ideas because they are afraid to act on them.

There is a story in the Bible where God told Joshua, the man who took over after Moses to tell the people of Israel to step out into the Jordan in order to create a way for them to pass. You can go through the scriptural passage in the book of Joshua 3. After personally going through this passage of scripture I realized that God demands courage from his people. You know it was one thing for God to open the red sea for the people to pass through after they had seen that it had opened, but it was a different experience altogether behind Jordan. This time, the Lord expected them to step into the river to create a path, and this was great risk. Do you know that the man who is without courage will easily withdraw from this? It takes courage to step into the unknown. Throughout my life and ministry, I have come across men and women who had ideas that could have changed the world. Ideas which would have helped solve most of the problems that exists in this world, had they been implemented. I knew a young man who had a great idea of business. The interesting thing about this young man was that he did not only have the idea, but he had a plan to achieving what he intended doing, yet he never did anything. Despite all his great ideas and plans, he lacked the courage to step out, and this led to his inability to do anything.

This is exactly what has happened to most gifted people out there. The same thing has also happened to most businesses, churches and other organizations which could have been bigger and greater than they are, had they the courage to make certain daring decisions. As a minister of the gospel, most of the major breakthroughs I had in my life came as a result of making courageous decisions and also taking courageous steps. I have come to realize that anytime I require courage to continue, then there is something big waiting. There are crusades and outreaches we were able to organize not because we had enough but we had the courage to do it. Every breakthrough, victory and triumph God will give you requires courageous steps to make it happen. God is always waiting for a courageous man to work with. I believe all those while that Goliath was chanting and abusing the people of God, He (God) was only waiting for someone who could step out in boldness and great courage to use in order to finish that talking philistine giant. But everyone was so afraid for their life that God had to wait a bit longer until a young anointed man full of courage appeared.

You cannot be a great man or woman of God if you are not a person of courage. Step out in courage today and see the wonders that will happen. Do not be afraid. There is nothing you cannot do if you choose to step out in courage. God is still telling his people to be bold and courageous, never to fear and they will see the good of the land. No wonder the disciples asked God to enable them to preach the gospel in boldness and great courage for they realized that miracles could not happen but through the act of courage. It is my prayer that as you read on, you will be emboldened and strengthened in courage to face anything in your life that may threaten to draw you away from your success, victory and breakthrough. There is nothing you cannot achieve if want to. There is nothing you cannot do when you step out in courage. That thing which is making you frightened and afraid to continue will fall before you if only you will not be afraid but instead muster the courage to approach it. God wants you to achieve greatness. He wants you to make it in your spiritual life, business and ministry. He wants the best for you in every aspect. Just step out in boldness and you will get there.

Fear Not

This statement actually appears several times in the Bible. It is believed that it appears about 365 times in the Bible, indicating that God wants us to be fearless each day of our lives throughout the year. This is because fear is a thief of success, victory and prosperity. A fearful individual amount to nothing in this life. Fear is the major cause of stagnation, retrogression and diversion. Fear is the greatest thief, killer and destroyer this world has ever known. Fear has caused confusion and wars, poverty and sicknesses, tragedies and deaths. It never wins. A fearful individual will never dare to do anything. He will sit at one place and die instead of daring to make a move that can change his or her life. Fear is the greatest killer this world has ever seen. Read this scripture Judges 7: 3, *"Now therefore go to, proclaim in the ears of the people, saying, whosoever [is] fearful and afraid, let him return and depart early from mount Gilead. And there returned of the people twenty and two thousand; and there remained ten thousand."*

I know this had to happen because fear does not fight but withdraws. It was very necessary for Gideon to eliminate all those who feared from amongst them if they were to win. I believe one of the reasons is that God wanted to prevent the other men from being affected, because fear can be very contagious. Fear never wins a battle. The Bible shows in Revelation 21:8 that the fearful is one of those who will be cast into the lake of fire. It is wrong to fear in the Kingdom of God. Every believer is born of the seed of God and as such He requires us to be bold and courageous. 2 Timothy 1: 7 says that, *"For God hath not given us the spirit of fear; but of power, and of love, and of a sound mind."* This is one of the reasons why you should not fear. God has invested much in giving you this character. The righteous shall be bold as a lion. Righteous men are bold in nature and not fearful.

There are lots of things we could have achieved if we had dared out in courage, but could not, because we were fearful. I believe lots of inventions; discoveries, ministries, companies and great businesses are still in the darkclutches of fear. Fear has brought great harm to our world than any other thing. Any fearful person easily becomes a slave to circumstances and situations.

Overcoming Fear

This is a very important thing every individual is expected to do if he will be able to achieve anything worthwhile in life. Until you are able to overcome your fears it will continue to paralyze you. The devil cannot succeed in your life until he is able to make you afraid. If he can make you afraid, then he can prevent you from achievement. Never forget this; the devil cannot stop you from moving forward in life. The best he can do is to try to make you stop yourself by making you afraid. Because the moment you become afraid, that fear itself will paralyze you.

One of the possible ways the devil can get access to your life is when you are afraid. Fear gives him entry. I believe that Job could have been safe had he not been afraid. The devil couldn't have had access, but for his fear. Let's read Job's own words in Job 3: 25-26 which says, *"For the thing which I greatly feared is come upon me and that which I was afraid of is come unto me. I was not in safety, neither had I rest, neither was I quiet; yet trouble came."* God cannot do much for the person who fears, until that individual overcomes his fears. God keeps telling us fear not, because fear is a great hindrance to success. As much as faith gives a man the ticket to access God, fear hinders any access to God. To really succeed every man needs to overcome what he fears. For man usually gets what he fears. Job was afraid of trouble, and that was what he got. What you fear will come upon you, if you don't overcome it. In other words, those who fear poverty become poor. This is because they are so afraid to take the steps that will get them out of poverty. The same thing happens to those who fear death too, they die. You indeed become what you fear, until you overcome your fear. And you can overcome all your fears. You can cease being afraid. Fearing is not so much an issue as not overcoming it is. All humankind has a habit of fear. Everyone has been afraid in one way or the other before. It is never true that courageous men do not fear.

Despite the great anointing on Jesus' life, there was one thing he feared – the cross. This was an issue he could only settle after fervent prayer. What you need to understand is that we all have our fears. Yet our greatest challenge does not lie in fearing, owing to the fact that everyone is afraid of something, but not confronting or overcoming our fears is the issue. The difference between winners and losers is that one has learned to overcome their fears whiles the other have not. Learn to master your fear, never allowing it to cripple you from making major strides towards achievement. John Wayne an American film actor, director and producer said, *"Courage is being scared to death … and saddling up anyway."* Nelson Mandela also quoted, *"I learned that courage was not the absence of fear, but the triumph over it. The brave man is not he who does not feel afraid, but he who conquers that fear."*

There have been times that I have been afraid in my life. I have faced very trying times that have made me very frightened and scared. But the art of confronting what we fear always helped me sail through. I once developed the habit of doing what I'm afraid to do, and this has been my formula for sailing through no matter the challenge I face. All the heroes and great generals of faith have come to the point of being scared to death before but what made them heroes was their ability to overcome their fears. Even David, on whose life these lessons are built became afraid in certain periods in his life. In Psalm 34: 4, he spoke about how the Lord delivered him from all his fears, indicating that he too feared sometimes.

Let us now look at the major types of fear which have crippled mankind from achievement and success throughout history and how they can be overcome. The main types of fear are *the fear of death, the fear of rejection, the fear of failure, the fear of criticism and the fear of poverty.* All others fall under these five. One would notice that for whatever thing any individual or group could not do or achieve one or more of these played a role.

1. The fear of death:

It has been said that it is risky not to take a risk, and this has proven to be true in all areas of life, whether in business, ministry or any other institution. All great achievements have been the result of great calculated risk. I have a friend whose life motto is, *'if you cannot risk it all, you cannot win it all,'* and he is a great fan of taking risks. If you want to win, then be prepared to be adventurous. You cannot be a high flyer if you don't brace yourself to making certain moves which might be risky. Risk taking is not negotiable if an individual wants to achieve heights in life. Even to be an effective follower of Jesus, you need to be prepared to risk everything to gain everything. Do you remember that Jesus told one Pharisee to go sell all he had, give it to the poor and come and follow Him? That is how it is in real life too. Risk taking has been a great part of the game of success and will always be part. And the fear of losing it all and not surviving is one of the things which have hindered most people from embarking any successful journey. It takes great act of courage to dare new heights and produce new results. New and profound results are achieved by risk takers. If you fear to lose your life for what you desire, then I'm sorry to let you know that you don't stand the chance of coming close to it.

The great men history produces are men who are prepared to die for their obsessions so much that they dare take any risk involved, no matter how perilous it seems. The simple advice the Bible gives to potential achievers is, 'to gain life, you must lose it.' Have you heard of the phrase, *"if I perish, I perish"*? This is commonly used by those who are willing to die for something. If you have not reached a crux where you are willing to die for what you want, then I think you are not yet obsessed with anything. And until what you want becomes an obsession you can't have it. It is said that some of the successful missionaries of old whose ministries were blessed with great revivals and awakenings were most of the time heard asking God to give them souls or they lose their lives in the process.

John Knox was so obsessed with the salvation of the whole Scotland that he was heard one-day agonizing in prayer demanding God to give him Scotland or take his life. And God also responded in grace, blessing Scotland with a widespread awakening. Men like John Hyde, a missionary sent to India in 1892 and George Whitefield were all heard, agonizing in prayers asking God to bless them with souls or else they die. These men had their various desires given them and were used by God to bring about major revivals in their time and this was because what they wanted had become an obsession so much that they were prepared to lose their lives for it.

Let me repeat this; until you want what you desire so bad that you are willing to lose it all to have it, you may not have it. Do you want that career, business, ministry or institution so bad that you are willing to lose all to have it? Everything is possible to achieve. All you need to do is want it so bad and then dare make the right move to have it. God feeds the hungry heart. The Bible says blessed are those who hunger and thirst, for they shall be filled. I know of a preacher of the gospel who went to God in prayer demanding a change of life until it happened. His option was for God to change his situation or else take his life and heaven responded.

The point I want you to get is not to go to God telling Him He should take your life if he is not going to bless you which brings the change, but defeating that fear which prevents people from stretching themselves to do what they need to do to produce the change they desire for fear of perishing whiles striving. Many people do not succeed because they do not really give their best shots in making their dreams come true. I heard the story of a billionaire who promised to give his daughter and a huge sum of money to any one of a group of men he selected who could swim his crocodile pool from one side to the other. After all the men withdrew on hearing the challenge, they heard splash in the water. They turned and saw one of them swimming and running as fast as he can in the pool as one running for his life. Many were surprised that this man could do that and survive. When asked what his motivation was, he exclaimed, still panting, that he didn't need any of those, all he wanted was to be shown the one who pushed him into the pool. I am sharing this story because of the truth it reveals. Most times we make discovery of our abilities when faced with dire situations of which we have to do everything to survive else we perish. All the other men were potential winners but withdrew and did not dare for fear of losing their lives in the process. That is the fear I am talking about.

There is also the story of an athlete who went to juju or vudu man to help him in an impending race competition he was going to participate. The juju man gave him a concoction to use before starting the race. He was to rub the substance in face before the race starts. On the day of the race he did just as directed and just when the race started, he saw a very big python after him. Not knowing what to do, he decided to run for his life, and by the time he realized everyone was cheering him up. He had won the race. Not understanding what he saw, he went back to the juju man for explanation. The man then told him that he had no medicine for making him first in the race, but knew that people give their best when under danger so as to survive. That was the formula he used on him.

You see many people retreat when the road they are plying to their destiny looks risky. Nobody was willing to take up the challenge of fighting Goliath because they knew what was involved. It was risky to fight Goliath due to his legacy and accolade in war. And it was seen by the army of Israel that any individual who would try might not survive, hence their retreat. Everyone was afraid of the situation even including King Saul and was not prepared to take any chances until David showed up. Golden opportunities normally show up in death threatening environments. And it is those who overcome that fear of death who get them.

Many people retreat from moving towards their destinies anytime they are afraid that something bad could happen whiles making a move. And this has crippled many people from pursuing any great feat in life. If you are afraid of taking risk then there is only one thing you are sure to achieve, and that is, nothing. Never forget that all major successes in life are not risk free. The best part of everything good is reserved for risk takers like Caleb and Joshua. Be bold and don't be afraid. Get up and dare new heights. There are still more lands to conquer and more discoveries to make. There is still room for you to rise to the top as a champion. Do not allow this fear of losing your life to stop you.

As much as I know there are life threatening experiences on the way to success, but don't be afraid. You won't lose your life so don't retreat. If God is for you, then He will keep you till you get to your destination. The devil will try to frighten you from pursuing your dream with death threatening scenes, but don't be afraid. Just be bold, and you will get through. Stop excusing yourself with that *"What if I don't survive,"* phrase and cease the opportunity when it comes. Don't build your life on such negative phrases like that. Be encouraged with a possible hope of survival and make a move. Instead of asking yourself "what if I don't survive," ask yourself "what if I survive" and then dare the journey to greatness.

One day the Jews were faced with a situation that needed the immediate intervention of God. They were about to be slaughtered by a man called Haman for selfish reasons. And they needed someone who could approach the king on their behalf so as to be saved. Queen Esther their only hope, who could have done the job easily, also harbored fear because it happened in a time where she could have lost her life even as a queen if she dared approach the king. But later, she decided to make the daring approach after waiting on God. *"If*

I perish I perish," Esther said, and by that act of courage great victory was won among the Jews (Esther 4-6).

He who wants to save his life for fear will lose it, but he who wants to lose his life will save it. What this piece of scriptural verse is saying is that, if you want to keep your life for fear of losing it in the process of any life changing act, you might end up losing it. And interestingly, those who dare to lose their lives for what they desire, do not lose it but save it at the end. Those who say if "I perish, I perish" do not really perish. But those who fear death instead die. The road to fulfillment is very frightening and risky so much that fearful men won't dare. Such was David's journey to the throne of Israel. His life was full of life threatening experiences to the extent that his own son wanted to take his life for the throne. King Saul also tried severally to spear him, but did not succeed. He made us aware that there were times he walked the valley of the shadow of death.

Many years ago, when the Lord was teaching me this lesson He showed me a dream. In the dream, I met my father standing at a junction with two different branch roads. When he turned, and saw me, I had opted for one of the branched roads, which was very narrow. Immediately he cautioned for me to stop. When I stopped, he started telling me about the dangers and risk on that road. He told me that if I choose that road I may not come back. But I insisted on plying that route since I believed that it led to my destiny. Do you know what? The journey was exactly as he said, but by the grace of Almighty God I survived every death attacks and came back safe and sound. When I made my return, I met him again at that same junction, and what shocked him was that I did not only come back but I returned with lots of goods and things that were impossible to carry. All he could say was that, 'so you came back?'.

I made a decision after I woke up that day not to allow anything to scare me in this life, and that I will not retreat no matter the challenges and difficulties including death treats I encounter on the road to achievement. I made the decision to dare the path that leads achievement and to live for purpose. This made me fearless before any challenge in this life. It was that day that I came to understand that my father was supposed to take that route himself but had been standing at that junction for fear of losing his life. This is what has happened to many people out there. They are standing at the junction of decision. It is not as if they do not know what they have to do and which path lead to their destination. They are very much aware of their callings, but what is preventing them is fear. What if we don't survive, they ask themselves?

It is an indisputable fact that the road to the impossible is never risk free. It is full of death threatening experiences, but if you will muster courage and move on, you will surely get to your destination. Will you say with the Psalmist, "Yea, though I walk through the valley of the shadow of death, I will fear no evil …" Hallelujah! Don't retreat from the valley of the shadow of death. Muster courage, walk through it and no harm shall come to you.Have you heard destiny calling out for you? Have you made the decision yet to pursue your calling or dream goal? Step out in faith, believing and trusting that you are not walking this path alone. The Lord is with you and will be with you throughout the journey, so fear not. Press on till you get to your intended destination, for that is why you are here.

2. *The fear of rejection*:

Do you know that much have not been achieved because of the fear of being rejected or ostracized? Most people have not dared anything towards the achievement of their destinies for the fear of being rejected should they make any move. Frankly speaking God never promised the removal of rejection anywhere in scripture but what the Psalmist assured us is that He takes us up when we are forsaken (Psalm 27: 10). For me, rejection is normal for any successful man. Every great dreamer will suffer rejection, especially when your dream contradicts the popular notion and expectation of those around you.

Many compromise their beliefs, opinions or ideas for fear of not being accepted, and are not able to share them. A lot more also compromise their living standards just to please others for fear of losing people. Do you know that peer pressure is the result of the fear of rejection? All victims of peer pressure do what they do to please their pals all for fear of losing friends. I realized early in life that people can stand many things in life but not rejection. Very few people have lived to overcome this. Those who live with this fear build their lives and emotions on other people's feelings and respond towards them. Their entire livelihood, happiness and fulfillment are dependent on external factors than internal factors. Their lives are built around what other people think or say about them.

If the people around them think their decisions are not right, then to them it is not right, and so will not pursue. They might have ideas or opinions that can change things or even improve their lives or the world, but the fact that it does not please those around them, they ignore it. Fear will not make you do anything, more especially this one. Many have thrown away innovative ideas, discoveries and inventions all because they were not welcomed by family and friends. Many have also ignored God's call because they were threatened or advised not to. I have come across people whose family rejected them for responding to God's call and also those who rejected God's call because family didn't agree to the idea.

Today there are lots of people out there in the world with ideas and solutions whose lives have amounted to nothing because they abandon any good idea which comes to them for fear of losing people. These are people who are always struggling for acceptance and are not able to live out their true self. Many people have not dared any uncommon feat in life because it might offend someone dear, and in other to avoid that they throw away what could have been a life changing moment for them. What I want you to understand is that if you fear rejection you can't achieve anything extraordinary. What matters in life are not what others think you should do but what you are convinced to do. Ignore what any ignorant folk is saying and pursue your dream. If they leave you, let them go, but concentrate on your dream and achieve it. It is normal to be rejected if you are a dreamer. I was once rejected for responding to the call of God. Joseph was rejected and later sold for dreaming. You will also be rejected for daring something big. This normally happens when the people around you start feeling that you are refusing their counsel. There are people today who are not happy in life because they chose the path those around them wanted them to go, for fear of being rejected and not what they were made to go. I read the story of a young man who graduated medical school with great honors come back home and handed over his certificate to his dad, and then asked his dad, if he could go and pursue his passion. When asked why, he said that being a doctor was his father's choice and not his. So, he did it for his dad, and now wanted to pursue his dream. There are several other people out there in life who never dared their dreams or destinies for fear of being refused and ostracized.

This is the simple reason why very few people climb up to the top in life. I tell you, it is better to suffer rejection and live in eternal happiness than to please men and live in confusion your whole life. It is by following your real passion that brings fulfillment and happiness. I am not saying rejection is a nice experience and I don't endorse it. But do not let it scare you to abandon your mission or calling. When men reject you for pursuing your destiny, God will receive you so don't be afraid. Let family, friends or even society ostracize you for what your life goal is, God won't.

One of the reasons I believe makes so many people run from rejection is mainly the feeling of loneliness it brings. Loneliness is not a nice experience and I also know that the Bible advices that it is not good. What you need to know is that God will never let you be or walk alone. He will neither leave you nor forsake you on the way. When those around you leave, He will bring others who can understand your calling and mission into your life to help you. If loneliness and solitude is what you fear, then take heart, because they also come with great benefits in the end.

Once a victim of rejection, I have come to know the blessings that come after rejection so much that I will easily embrace it anytime it comes. Most great achievers were victims of rejection. The bible is full of the rejection stories of Moses, Joseph, Jephthah and David. At one time, David's father had forgotten about him, until the prophet Samuel asked if he had any more sons. That was when he remembered he had a son who was far away. Have you been in the position where because you chose to follow God or your dream, you were rejected by family, friends and society? If you have been there before, did you notice that you were never alone? Did you notice that when you chose to stick to your God given dream, that was when God revealed His presence in your life? Rejection brought me more closely to God than anything. For me it is one of the greatest advantages I have had in life.

It was through rejection that I understood the power of solitude. The Lord used these periods of rejection to teach me lots of things I didn't know. Do not be afraid that you will lose people when you choose to do the right thing. When all leave, God will not leave you. He will be with you right from the beginning to the end. Don't quit but keep doing the right thing. Don't try keeping those who want to leave. Let them go, because if you don't, you will end up regretting later on. People mostly leave us in this case when they do not understand what we are doing but that should not make you change your mind. If they will leave you because you chose to do the right thing, let them go. Just don't give up. God will not desert you. Only keep moving and you will make it. Do not let the fear of rejection cease you from pursuing your dream. When everybody rejects you, don't reject yourself. When all people shun you, don't be disappointed. God will never leave you nor forsake you. He will be your help, guide and rock till you get to your destination. He is right there at the valley of decision waiting for you to come so that

He would walk with you through the paths of adventure. Make that daring move which can turn things around in your life. He wants to do the impossible with you. He wants to take you deeper and higher, only be bold and courageous. Make the decision, step out, and you will see the good of the land.

3. *The fear of failure or making a mistake*

This is another type of fear that has wrecked great havoc to humanity. One of the great dangers of fear is that it is a thief, killer and destroyer. Fear has killed millions of lives, dreams and ideas. Many people had good ideas which would have changed the world had they been implemented, but for the fear of failure, those ideas were never born but remained hidden. A certain man had a wonderful idea of starting his own gasoline filling station. He had mapped out all plans to get this going until one day another man discouraged him. He asked him, "what if this plan fails?" Though this was a short question; it was enough to discourage him, because he became so frightened at losing his investment if his plan did not work, and as a result never tried that idea.

If you fear failure, you will fail. This is because you will never try anything new for fear of failing. Those who succeed are never terrified at failing or making mistakes, and as a matter of fact they don't give up when they fail. Winston Churchill said, "Success is the ability to move from failure to failure without losing enthusiasm." If you get discouraged and give up because you failed, you may never achieve anything. Those who fear failing in life, live to fail all their lives. Almost all successful people have failed before, whereas all champions in life have once been defeated before. Most winners once had temporary defeats, so don't be scared.

Sir Thomas Edison is one of the men who shall be remembered on this planet for his ability to persist and continue trying and failing about thousand times when he decided to work on the electric bulb.

The electric bulb that we enjoy today is evident that failing is only an option, and that if anyone persists, success will be attained. I can go on and on talking about men and women who once failed yet chose not to give up but pushed through and with dedicated and focused efforts, persisted until they finally achieved their dream goal. If someone didn't give up failing for the thousand counts, why should you give up at the first?

Let your failures be your stepping stone to your pending victories. Let failure encourage you and don't allow it to discourage you. If you fail the first time, don't worry. No one is expecting you to get it right at the first time, or even second and third times. If you get it right at the first time, bless God and continue. And if you get it wrong at the first time, don't put pressure on yourself and quit. Also, bless God, learn from your mistakes and continue till you achieve what you want. One of these days I suggest that you try and study how a child learns to walk. No matter the number of times the child falls or fails trying to walk, he or she does not stop but continue trying until he masters the art of walking. Failure is not a signal of stop, but a signal of "try it some more".

Most educated folks developed this fear of failure right from school days, where getting wrong answers is not advisable and accepted. I remember in my school, you dare not get an answer wrong. Because getting an answer wrong merited different punishments. You were either rewarded with low grades, scolded and get contempt from teachers and peers. So, with this almost everyone try to avoid failure at any cost, including not trying anything due to the unpleasantness and seeming shame that comes with it.

In some schools in Africa, where punishing students is seen as advisable, students receive strokes of lashes for failing. No one wants to fail, and to avoid the embarrassment that came from failure, some never dared answer or ask any question. I had a friend in my school days that stopped trying to answer questions in class because he was always scolded anytime he got answers wrong whenever he attempted. This fear of being mocked drove him to stop attempting to solve problems. This is what happens to most people when they enter real life. They stop trying when they fail at the first time. Others too do not start anything at all for fear of failing at the first time. And this has been a big damage to the progress of most.

Please understand that you cannot break forth into better results and performance if you are harboring this fear. Don't be afraid of failing. That case in school is not the same in real life. Any successful person in business will tell you that the fastest way to succeed is to first jump in, make things happen and be okay with failing repeatedly. The saying "Fail fast and fail often" is a popular statement you might probably hear from the entrepreneurial circle. You need to learn to embrace failure as soon as possible, get corrected by learning from mistakes and forge on using your failure as a stepping stone.

If you have experienced failure in any way, don't be afraid. Keep trying, don't give up yet, and you will surely get to your goal. Failure is not the falling down but the staying down, and it is a choice. Don't stay down, get up, put yourself together and try again. Let success be your only option, and then work at it till you get to your intended destination. Do not let the fear of failure grip you. Let the failure you encounter be to you as a temporary defeat and encourage yourself. The number of times you have failed does not matter. Just get up and move on. You have fallen and so what. Who told you that falling is final? Have you not read that, a just man falls seven times, but rises again seven times? You can fall the seventh time and still be a just man – you still carry in you the potential to be great, so get back up.

For a just man falleth seven times, and riseth up again (Proverbs 24: 16).

Show me a man who claims he has not fallen before, and I will show you a man who will never rise if he falls. *Even a tree has hope that when it is cut down, it will sprout out again and that the tender branch will not cease* (Job 14:7). If you fear making mistakes, you will never try anything new. There is a quote that says, "The man who claims he has never failed before, has never tried anything new." If you fear falling, you will never try walking. Any child who never tries walking, for fear of falling will remain lame until it sheds off that fear and tries using its legs. I know students who could have become good academically but never became, for fear of being laughed at when they make mistakes.

I also know men who could have become great healing ministers, but for fear of failing, they never tried ministering healing to anybody. 'What if it does not work,' most ask themselves. You see I am here talking as one who has been a victim of this before. Have you tried ministering healing to the sick before? If yes, did you take notice of the thoughts that flooded your mind when you attempted it? That is what I am talking about. The next time you hear those thoughts ringing in your mind, also ask yourself what if it works, and focus on making it happen, and it will happen. Do not let failure stop you from doing anything. It is better to try it and fail than to try doing nothing. After all, the one who tried and failed has a great advantage over the one who never tried anything. At least he can tell you how an approach won't work by his failure.

4. *The fear of what others will say or criticism*

Emerson once said, *"Whatever course you decide upon, there is always someone to tell you that you are wrong. There are always difficulties arising that tempt you to believe your critics are right. To map out a course of action and follow it to an end requires some of the same courage that a soldier needs. Peace has its victories, but it takes brave men and women to win them."* There are always going to be people who will criticize any course of action whether good or bad. You have to understand that critics are everywhere and that whatever a man chooses to do, he will be criticized. Just as Jesus Christ was criticized, the same way, you will you also be criticized. Most good men encountered great criticism for what they believed. No man or woman of honor was free from criticism. Anytime you choose to do something different, great criticism awaits you, some constructive and others destructive.

The Wright brothers got their share of criticism when they discussed their fledging idea of making the airplane. No matter how Americans Idolize Abraham Lincoln, he was one of the most criticized presidents in the history of America. He was criticized and abused almost on all fronts despites his inputs and achievements, even by his home people. Dr. Kwame Nkrumah a renowned African president was one of the most criticized presidents of his days, despite the fact that he is celebrated today. The truth about most critics is that they jump on you when they don't know anything about what you are doing. Ignorance is one of the major causes of criticism.

The moment you envision doing something different, you must also be prepared to be met with criticisms. This world is such that when you choose to be an impact maker or an achiever, there will be people on the way who will try talking you out of it. If you fear to be criticized, you will never step out. People are always talking, and people will always talk. If you don't want to be criticized, then stay ordinary. But if your dream is to make a mark, then ignore your critics and pursue your dream. Those who criticize are always behind. It is true that not all our critics mean harm. Some criticisms are very constructive and are meant to help us get the right things done but others are very destructive. Most people will criticize you when they are threatened by your level of competence, attractiveness or even success. Others too criticize you when they don't understand your vision or thus feel. Those who criticize for the right reasons do so genuinely to help you benefit from their wisdom and experience. Also, know that others will criticize you when your actions bring them hurt or even disadvantage them. Yet in all these, what you should understand is never to allow criticisms whether good or bad to stop you from pursuing your dream goal. Just leave your critics to do their job. Learn from those you should learn from and ignore those that are not useful to you then move on to pursue your dream.

Most critics do not know or understand what you are doing. After all, they don't see what you see. You are the carrier of that vision. You are the only person who understands what you have seen. So, concentrate on it, investing all efforts and resources into making it happen. Most of the inventions and good things we see around were all born out of great criticism. Don't waste precious time arguing with your critics or try to explain what you are doing to them; they are not ready to agree with you. Listen to wise counsel and get busy with your work. It is best to impress God and not people. The successes you are working at will one-day manifest so don't give up.

Had I not learnt early in life to close my ears to most of the negative things people were saying, I wouldn't have come this far. There were times too I listened to some of the criticism that came, learned from them and carried on. Never did I allow the criticism I encountered to distract me in any way. No one is happy at being criticized. There are times you get broken when you hear the things people are saying about you. There had been times like that in my life too. Times that I felt like reacting or throwing back at my critics, but then later choose to ignore and carry on. Abraham Lincoln's wife revealed how the criticisms he encountered caused him great pain.

She said at times after hearing some of these, Lincoln is heard saying he would rather be dead than, as president, abused in the house of his friends. Yet it is said that he responded to the flood of naysayings with a weary wave of his hand and say, "Let us speak no more of these things." Today the world celebrates him for his efforts and achievements, and ranks him as one of the greatest presidents in the history of America.

This book belongs to those who are ready to change the course of history and influence this world for good. I mean those who are ready to occupy till Jesus comes, just as He suggested. If you have a dream you want to achieve or are on your way to fulfilling your destiny, keep on and don't be afraid of what the people are going to say. As much as it is good to listen, also don't forget that, not all the words and comments from people are worth listening. Most of these are meant to discourage or distract you, but don't give in or allow them to. Only give ears and attention to those people whose words and comments can be a great boost to success, those whose aim is to help you succeed. There are people we owe our success to. Their comments and counsel fueled my system to perform. Men like Apostle Emmanuel Adade, Bishop Charles Agyin Asare, Bishop Dag Heward Mills and several others have been of great inspiration and great help.

There are lots of things God wants to do through you. Forget about what people will say and move out. What matters is the thing the Lord is saying about you. Do not give the devil this chance of ensuring that other people stop you from progressing. Has the Lord impressed any idea on your heart? Is He urging you to make a life changing step? Do not be afraid. The Lord is with you. He will help you and make sure that you get to your destination safely, if only you will heed to what He is saying.

5. *The fear of Poverty*

It is mostly believed that this particular fear is the deadliest and has caused the world much harm than the other forms. Of all the ages of the world of which we know anything, the age in which we live seems to be the age of money worship. A man is considered less or unimportant unless he can display a fat bank account. Today in most countries, especially Africa, there are lots of good things you cannot do if you are poor. In a world where the poor is easily intimidated and abused, nothing brings man so much suffering and humiliation as does POVERTY. No wonder man fears poverty. Today, the weak is easily trampled by the strong, the poor the richer, the sick the healthier and the disabled the abled.

I know a man who owned a great vast land in a village close to the town I live, but that property was taking over by someone of great substance and nothing was given to him. When I heard this story the only thing that came to my mind was the story in the Bible, where King Ahab and his wife Jezebel took over Naboth's vineyard against his wish and killed him (1King 21:1-16). This is what always happens in this world. The mighty easily trample the weak. It has always been that same story; the fittest survives. In our world, today, poor men rarely get justice. There is a big gap that separates the rich from the poor, and interestingly it has entered the church of God too.

Today in most churches, there are seats specially kept for men of substance, while the poor have where they sit too. The rich men in our churches today receive special treatment, whereas the poor is often abused. Our leaders always advice the people to educate their wards, which is a great suggestion, but let's be frank and ask the percentage of the population who gets access to quality education. This is because it is very expensive now. Do you also know that most marriages have their beginnings (and oftentimes their endings) solely on the basis of the wealth possessed by one or both of the contracting parties?

In his book, the law of success Napoleon Hill remarked that today "Society" could quite properly be spelled "$ociety," because it is inseparably associated with the dollar mark. In a world where some have been made to feel inferior and others superior all because of poverty, no one wants to have anything to do with poverty. I remember asking this question while speaking in a conference, 'who wants to be poor,' but I had no response. I then went on to ask 'who wants to be rich,' there I saw every hand up. I recently saw a television program, titled 'Who wants to be rich.' and it looked interesting. Why do you think people use such names or titles to brand the programs they do?

No one wants to be poor, for fear of being down trodden or disrespected. Due to this many never dare their destinies for fear of never becoming rich or never achieving any financial success. So instead of following their passion, they resort to short cut means of getting money. I remember someone coming to me to ask if I would ever be rich or make any financial stride doing the work of God. He asked, "Will you ever be rich doing this?" You see this is what scares people away from going after their heart. Probably yours might not be someone asking but you asking. You have to understand that one of the main reasons why people follow their passion is not for the money but the joy and happiness it brings them and others as well as impacting other lives positively, though most get rich at the end. It will interest you to know that most of the richest men in history followed after their passion to the extent that some dropped out of school to pursue what they loved doing.

Always those who risk their lives to follow after their passion are compensated with wealth if they don't give up despite their uncertain and doubtful beginnings. Do not throw your gifting and abilities away because you are in a haste to get rich. Do not make hasty judgments considering people's beginnings. Don't be afraid. Allow yourself to be tutored and developed, and then go after what you were made to be. You won't be poor so don't be discouraged. It is true that the journey to achieving destiny is not an easy one but do not be despaired. There is great fortune awaiting you. Only dare this path that leads to your destiny. Do not be part of those men who are so eager to possess wealth at all cost through whatever means available, whether legal or illegal. Men who cheat, steal, commit murder, engage in robbery and all other manner of violation of the rights of others just to bring them wealth and riches or gain more of it. Dare to be different and you won't be poor. Do not let that fear of poverty drive you to be part of corrupt practices. The fear of poverty is perceived to be one of the reasons why corruption is rampant in the world today. Everyone wants to escape the shame and ridicule poverty brings, hence the rush to make wealth whether in a good or bad way.

Do not be deceived to use evil means to get wealth. You are already born for wealth and prosperity. God has already made provisions for your success in Christ Jesus. His word says in the book of 3John 1:2, ***"Beloved I wish above all things that thou mayest prosper ..."*** He wants you to prosper and be influential, so don't resort to evil ways of acquiring wealth. Be informed and you will perform. Fear not, for God in His wisdom has made available every wealth and riches you would need in Christ Jesus. Just seek first the progress of His Kingdom and every other good thing shall be added. God is not interested in your poverty either, and is prepared to help you out of it. Only follow His ways and leading and you will be full of abundance. Trust in the Lord with all your heart. Do not lean on your own understanding of things. Do your best to acknowledge God in all your ways and He shall direct your path to the place of abundance.

How to Overcoming Fear

Remember that it was said that courage is not the absence of fear, but conquering it. All great men have been afraid or frightened about something in their lives before. Through hereditary (whether social or biological) every man has either one of the forms fear. What makes some great and some ordinary is that, those who become great men put up actions that enable them to overcome their fears, whiles ordinary men are overcome by fear. Until you learn how to overcome your fear, you will be hindered by your fear forever. Fear is a great thief of success and is one of the major causes of retrogression, stagnation and diversion in this life. Whereas courage will give a man access to his God-given land, fear will hinder you from enjoying all God has prepared for you. History shows that nothing good has ever happened to those who fear.

The story of the people of Israel is a great example of how, fear can hinder a man from progress and cause him to suffer in life. Fear was the reason why Jonah fled from going to Nineveh to do the bidding of the Lord. Sincerely speaking, most of our arguments with God against doing His will are due to fear. All God wants us to learn doing is to overcome fear everyday of our lives, so that we will be able to fulfill our destiny. The word of God admonishes us severally not to be afraid. This implying that no matter what forms our fear is, it can be overcome. You can overcome that fear of death, criticism, rejection, failure and of poverty. Like Joshua and Caleb, we know that we are not alone, and that we are able to conquer every fear which besets us from success.

If God be for us, what can be against us? Is it death, peril, persecution, hunger, nakedness, loneliness, trouble or adversity? Nothing can separate us from what we believe, brethren in the Lord. For in all these we are more than conquerors through Christ who loves us. Hallelujah! No believer is meant to be a victim or loser. We have been designed to possess abilities that equip us to overcome every frightening situation in our lives which has the ability to draw us from victory or success. Below are seven points that will help you overcome your fears:

1.   *Trust in the Lord, your strength*:

Understand that you are never alone in this life no matter your situation. God is always there for those who feel lonely and dejected. That is why the Bible uses terms like father of the fatherless and husband of the widow for God. This shows that God is always ready to keep you company whether you know it or not. His promise is for you not to be afraid because he won't leave. He is not only with you to keep you company but also to strengthen and empower you for victory. Do not be overwhelmed by the challenges you get to face in life. God will see you through it all without any harm.

Do you know why though the people of Israel were few, compared to other kingdoms of the world, yet they did totally impossible things? Read Psalm 78 to know most of those things which happened among them. The truth is that God was their strength and power. Prophet Samuel, in 1 Samuel 15:29, referred to Him as the Strength of Israel. It says,

"And the strength of Israel will not lie nor repent."

This was what the Psalmist also believed when he wrote Psalm 27:1. It says, **"Lord is my light and salvation, whom shall I fear; the Lord is the strength of my life of whom shall I be afraid"**.

Trust in all His Word and promises to you and you will never be ashamed. No wonder that those who trust in the Lord shall be unmovable like Mount Zion. If the Lord is your strength, then there is nothing you cannot do. No height shall be impossible to reach. No mountain of hindrance can stop you from progressing for the Spirit of God will see you through.

2. Learn to take action

Your trust in God should lead you into action. Action takers are conquerors of fear. Taking action is one of the surest way to overcome fear. Do what you fear doing, and you will gradually end the fear of doing that thing in your life. God never took what men and women feared away but always gave them the strength and courage to do the same things they feared. He gave Esther that courage to approach King Ahasuerus, which led to the emancipation of her own people in that land of slavery. He will always strengthen you to do what you are afraid of. The more you do what you fear, the easier it becomes for you to do that particular thing. Learn to take action or do whatever you are afraid to do, because that is the surest way to overcome your fears.

Chapter 3

DEVELOP A STRONG FIGHTING SPIRIT

"...and a man of war ..." 1Sam 16: 18

There is this popular notion about life as a battle field. Well I don't doubt that. But all I can say for now is that this life is never a playground. In order to rise to the top in any field of endeavour, you have to know how to fight your way through. In the jungle, the best fighter is King and so is this world. One thing I think most believers need to understand is that Jesus never died and rose to change conditions in this world. He did this to change us and empower us to go through this life. We will also meet what the people of this world meet, on their way to achievement. But in all this our story should be different. I will go deeper on this later. But the truth I want you to understand is that, in this life we meet all sought of things that seek to hinder us from progress and success, and to be able to sail through to higher heights in any field of endeavor, you need to develop a strong fighting spirit.

This explains why many have been victimized. If you have encountered people in every walk of life, I think you would understand what I am talking about. The reason why people try all sought of means to get emancipated from most of the woes of this life is the result of the constant battles life presents. All across the pages of social history, there is one thing you don't cease to see or notice, that is, many have been whipped by certain issues of life and have been left brutalized and victimized. As a minister of the gospel I have always witnessed the stories of people who seem to be crushed and totally disintegrated due to one issue or the other which happened to them in this life.

People have come to me weeping and groaning over issues and matters of life. Get to churches and other religious groups and you will see people who bear scars and marks of different issues seeking answers for the problems, troubles and challenges each day brings. You see, God has not promised anywhere in His Word an easy ride through this life. What He promises is the assurance of getting through any situation or difficulty no matter what. He most often uses those things we go through to develop us and train our hands for battle. God knows best and helps us understand later that we really needed those challenges or battles so as to get to our intended destinations in life.

That is why in the book of Judges 3:1-2, the Bible says, "...*these are the nations which the Lord left, to prove Israel by them, even as many of Israel as had not known all the wars of canan; Only that the generations of the children of Israel might know, to teach them war, at least such as before knew nothing thereof.* He God, left other opposing Canaan nations undefeated, so that through them He could teach each generation of Israelites war. The Contemporary English Version of the Bible puts the same verse this way, *"And the LORD had another reason for letting these enemies stay. The Israelites needed to learn how to fight in war, just as their ancestors had done. Each new generation would have to learn by fighting."* The Psalmist also said, *"Blessed be the LORD my strength, which teacheth my hands to war, and my fingers to fight"* Psalm 144: 1. You need to know and learn how to fight your way through to your destiny, and God will help you do that if you give Him the chance. There are certain enemies which can hinder you from getting close to your breakthrough which need to be defeated. To be successful you need to defeat those enemies of ignorance, disappointment, discouragement, despair, distractions, disloyalty and indiscipline. Defeat these and you are sure to find your way to success, and to do that you need to have a fighting spirit. Interestingly every believer has this ability in his or her spirit but is undeveloped.

To develop that attitude of a fighter, God takes us through series of challenges (which doesn't come from Him necessarily). Each of us needs both the spiritual and psychological muscles to fight our way through. I know that the setbacks, challenges and resistance which we face are all to build in us the strength and wisdom we need to get to our destinations. Strength grows out of resistance. This is not to say that all challenges come from God;most are self-imposed whereas others are from the devil. There are some too God allows into our lives to help develop us for our destiny. This was the main reason why God took the people of Israel through the wilderness before leading them into the Promised Land.

If you lack the strength and energy to fight on your way to success, then you have a long way to go. If you care to know there is no easy means to greatness in life, yet it doesn't mean you should settle down for anything less. Live for something uncommon, and be bold to fight till you achieve it. Let nothing neither terrify nor stop you. Develop that spirit of a fighter in you, if only you want to do the impossible. Men of faith are really men of war. They have the ability to fight their way through to the top. If you see men who have genuinely risen in their field of endeavors, respect and pay them 'tribute'. This is because not all are able to sail through the challenges of life. They need your respect for surviving and overcoming what hinders others.

Great men are really over comers. You cannot be termed a champion, if you have not won any battle or challenge. An over comer is someone who has overcome. A victor has also won. And they do these by fighting. Great rewards are given to those who overcome.

Read the book of Revelation 2, 3 and you will realize how Christ himself cherishes over comers.

David became an outstanding man among his peers, because he had a great fighting spirit. Even at a tender age he had some victories under his belt. He looked younger, youthful and naturally unqualified for the job at hand, but he had the spirit of a fighter, which is what mattered. He was a youth on the outside but a man of war already on the inside.

What normally qualifies people for battle is not necessary physical structure but internal stature. It looks nice to have well-built men in the army but if they are not well built on the inside; your army won't have any future. This is because true strength comes from the inside and not on the outside. If you have been to a military training ground before, what you will realize is that those trainings are not just meant for their outward development but more importantly their inward development. Men of war are made on the inside than on the outside. Isn't it just amazing when someone who had spotted David and knew he wasn't a military man start calling him a man of war? At the time, David was not even yet the military age, which was age 20 then. Does that mean that you don't need to be in the army to be a man of war? Exactly! Men of war possess an extra ordinary strength on the inside. What I want you to understand is that you do not need huge muscles to be a fighter; all you may need is a well-developed internal and psychological muscles.

That was what David had. Nothing can stop such a man. Not even the Goliath of life. Aren't you amazed at how David handled Goliath's case? It was just a spectacle. This was not a military man handling his enemy but a man of war dealing with issues; it was a man with a strong fighting spirit putting things in their right place.

I use to wonder how that servant of King Saul who recommended David knew what David was made of. Because all this while David was a sheep tender, a wilderness boy, and unknown. Yet this servant knew somehow that he was a man of war, though he had not seen him fight in any war. This should tell you that there is more to being a man of war we need to know. Men of war are known for their adventures in real life. Most times, it is not just about the fight, but what the fight leaves in you that matters. How come someone is called a man of war when he had not yet fought in any battle? I believe that his experiences in the wilderness had built in him a great fighting spirit which was demonstrated in his daily life. It is not just enough to have started something, build that capacity that will help you get through to the end. To conquer and win in this life, you need to have this fighting spirit. You need to be a fighter to get through this life. Did you notice the direction God gave Gideon in order that he could get the finest and the actual men of war? After that hosts of fearful men were separated, the next thing was to take the rest to that place where he could separate those who were men of war from those who were not. How do you know that someone is a man of war? And, what makes them men of war? Men of war are fighters in attitude than in aptitude.

Our Fight

"Fight the good fight of faith ..." 1 Timothy 6:12

In the Old Testament, men and kingdoms fought, but our fight is not with men (Ephesians 6:12). Today we fight to overcome imaginations, reasoning, ideologies and suggestions from those things we face on the way to achievements or from evil forces of darkness which seek to hinder us from progressing to our intended ends or destinies. There are lots of challenges, difficulties and very trying times on our way to achieving excellence. We face hurts, accusations, criticisms, oppositions, slander, scorn, betrayal, disappointments, depression and even oppression either from humans or from negative forces any time we make a move towards destiny. The journey to achievements as commonly known is neither smooth nor simple. The simplest route in life leads to nothing. Therefore, he who is not prepared to face anything should opt for nothing. But if any man is ready to achieve any great feat in life, then he should prepare for different battles on the way. The road to achievement is full of both rough and smooth moments, as well dry and wet seasons. Have you ever asked yourself why not all become great in life, though, everyone can be great? Have you asked why very few people in society make it to the top or fulfill their actual calling? As a minister of the gospel, I know and understand why some begin the Lord's work genuinely but later on divert or deviate from their true calling. This life is full of battles of all kinds and to make it to the top you need to be able to fight your way through to the top with the help of God. No one is crowned a winner until he has won a particular fight. Neither is anyone crowned a champion until he wins his lot.

Hear me; you are not an overcomer until you have been able to overcome. I believe heaven will be greatly relished by those who could overcome the battles of life on earth. Jesus in His seven letters to the churches in Revelation 2 took time to show overcomers their portion in heaven. You need to learn to overcome in order to book your place among champions. The truth is that, there are adverse times ahead on the road to fulfillment. You emerge a champion if you are able to fight your way through this. Did you realize what David had to go through before ascending the throne? One would imagine why it should be this way in our lives.

Why do I have to go through all that to be able to ascend the throne of promise? Why is it so important for God to take us through adverse times, before we are established? The issue is that God is not just interested in taking us up, but also establishing us up there when we get there. He thus takes time to develop our abilities, gifts, talents and also to develop the right attitude and character in us. He is able to bring the best out of us during adverse and challenging times, and not in times of comfort. And for this to happen, we need to bear with Him as He leads us through these times and moments of development so as to produce in us that spiritual and psychological muscles we need to advance to our land of promise.

This story is told of a man who heard God spoke to him one day whiles praying. The Lord told him He loved him and that He had great plans for him. He told him He wanted to do wonderful things with him in his nation and beyond, to which the man gladly agreed and accepted. One day as he prayed, the Lord visited him again, and this time gave him an assignment to do for Him. The Lord showed him a very huge rock which stood in front of his house, and told him his assignment was to push it. After this man agreed to do it, he gladly began the next day. After a year of rock pushing, and seeing no results, he finally became discouraged and nearly gave up, but on a second thought, he decided to go back to the Lord in prayers.

Our merciful God appeared to him again after his many complaints and accusation in prayer, and asked him what his problem was. Then he said if God really loved him why did He give him such a useless task to do, when God Himself knew it was impossible, for he has pushed the rock for over a year and has not been able to move it. On hearing this, the Lord burst out in laughter, shaking His head anytime He looked at the man. The man, surprised at why God was laughing, angrily shouted, "Why are you laughing at me." Then God told him, "I never told you to move the rock but to push it, and that is what you have been doing over one year now. Again, who told you that it is useless and that you have not benefited. Remove your shirt and check your muscles, were they like this a year before." Then the man answered, "no". So, the Lord told him that that was exactly what he wanted him to have before He would send him

For us, we do not necessarily need to build up big physical muscles, but rather psychological. To be able to get through to attain any goal in this life we need some mental toughness, great wit and will power and mastery of our emotions. Anyone who lacks these barely survives. This is quite the reason why many give up plying the road of success. You need a strong fighting spirit to finish the race on this earth. The character or attitude of a warrior is very needful for both your spiritual, psychological and physical survival, so give time to developing it. Paul knew what he was doing when he likened the believer to a soldier. (Read my book, The Blessings of Adversity for more detail on this topic). Below are some qualities of a true fighter you need to develop in order to succeed:

1. Endurance

"Thou therefore endure hardness, as a good soldier ..." 1 Timothy 2: 3

Endurance is the ability or capacity to withstand hardship or stress. It is that stay power that keeps an individual going in any given situation whether in the midst of pain and difficulty. To succeed you need this ability. There is no easy way or shortcut to success or breakthrough in this life, and while you travel the road to success, you will meet situations seemingly overwhelming which will try to put you off or hinder you from advancing. Endurance will help you sustain over time, to call from ourselves renewed commitment and effort when we are confronted with challenges or hardship. Endurance often requires tolerating needful discomfort, and may call on us to reach for resources and stamina we are not certain we possess.

Endurance means that we remain steadfast even through criticism, monotony, and discouraging odds. As we have already learned, this life is not free of adversity. The Bible already assures us that very difficult times shall come in the last days, so it is not new. Each man will meet adverse times and seasons as he walks the path that leads to greatness whether rich or poor, black or white. The only difference is that winners stay on in such times and that is what takes them far. There is a popular saying that heroes are like everybody, but they are only able to endure five minutes longer. Historian George Kennan said "**Heroism is endurance for one minute more.**"

This was what Paul; the apostle was revealing to Timothy who was an up and coming general for God's kingdom in the verse above. He wanted him to understand that every good soldier must have the ability to endure hardness since anything can happen on the battlefield. I know some of you will best understand this only when they become soldiers. There is nothing like a champion without endurance. Have you noticed that every general or commander of an army has some batch or ropes around their shoulders? The number of ropes shows your rank in the army. That is exactly how it is in real life. Real life also puts ropes around the shoulders of champions in any field, and there is no doubt that one of those ropes is endurance. No one can fake heroism in real life. You will be exposed by the time you realize. If you can endure, then you have a great opportunity to succeed wherever you go, because there is nothing you cannot go through. History shows that most of the great men life has produced endured series of traumas to get to where they are. They endured shame, hunger, peril, persecution, poverty and various disasters which came their way. The victory came when they chose to hold on where others gave up. The Bible puts it this way: "...*he that endures to the end shall be saved*" (Matthew 10:22). If you can hold on a little longer, you will notice that you are not far from the victory. The Lord has great things in stock for you. His plan concerning your life is awesome and will bring you to a greater end. God's chief aim for working tirelessly in your life is to make you the head in what you do. Just hold on a little longer. That issue which is troubling you is temporal and will not last.

2. Focus

"No man that warreth entangleth himself with the affairs of this life ..." 2 Timothy 2:4

"Soldiers on duty don't work at outside jobs," this is how the Contemporary English Version puts it.

What this means is that a soldier does not entertain distractions in every way. One of the few attributes that marks a good soldier is the art of focus and concentration. Focus is the state of staying off distractions and concentrating on a chosen goal or task, making it a center of interest till the end. It is also committing one's self to a given goal or work until success is achieved. Soldiers on duty have only one main point of interest, and that is their responsibility or task set for them. They don't mingle civilian issues with military issues. Focus is a very important recipe for success. I can boldly tell you that, you cannot make any remarkable impact if you don't focus on your dream goal. Though it is not the only virtue or character prerequisite for success, it is one of the most important virtues which ensure success.

There has never been any story of greatness or achievement told about any individual, without that individual having to do without focus. To succeed in any given field of endeavor and become one of the best, you need to develop the art of concentration on whichever goal set before you. Never forget that every great performance that ever happened in the past always required a great deal of concentration. If you can't concentrate, you can't penetrate. To succeed, one of the things to stay off is allowing things that are distractive in nature to take your attention. Distractions are the things that make it difficult for one to pay attention or commit to one thing. Distractions are the thieves of progress. They steal or hinder your effectiveness in any field of endeavor.

In anything a man sets his heart to do, there are always things which can easily distract him. This life is full of distractive things. *"Work is hard. Distractions are plentiful. And time is short,"* said Adam Hochschild. Concentrating on a given goal amidst all the distractions around is a very important key to success. One of the reasons why many people or organizations are never able to achieve success is their inability to focus. It always pays to focus, though it is not that simple or easy to focus. When a man uses his concentration power well, mighty wonders happen. I once got glued to a movie many years ago, where

I realized one of the simplest lessons of concentration. A monk was having a meditational prayer, when a mosquito started biting and sucking his blood. The interesting thing here which got me wondering is that he never moved, neither did he stop praying despite the pain. I didn't cease thinking about this whole meditational thing I saw, until I got the lesson in it.

Despite the pain that man might have felt, he kept his cool until he finished his prayer. The things that can distract you are attractive, nice and very enticing in nature. I believe if it is not attractive or deeply felt, then it cannot distract. Distractive things are always tempting. The types of things which easily get people off their goal, dream or vision come as very nice and lucrative opportunities. I am talking about those lucrative business, educational or life opportunities which are not part of your original goal, dream or vision. The one who can focus amidst all the things which could lure him or her to lose concentration is the one who gets ahead in every given field.

Let me say this; it is easy to be distracted, and as a matter of fact anybody can be distracted. Those who are able to stay focus are not from another planet. They are just like everybody. The only difference is that they learn and discipline themselves to get committed to what they are doing. Learn to stay focus to your goal and you will be rewarded. There are also people who get distracted at the slightest disappointment or pain. There are others too who get discouraged when they face challenges or troubles. Get your eyes fixed on what you want to achieve and never take your eyes off until you achieve it. I have come across people who could have achieved great feats in what they were doing had they focused and concentrated, but instead allowed challenges to change their directions to different things.

There are people who jump from one thing to the other at the slightest disadvantage. They don't finish with what they start before shifting to something different. They want to do anything that comes into their mind, and as a matter of fact do not concentrate on one thing; hence their failure to achieve anything great in this life. Sometimes it is so worrying when you ask people what they would like to do or be, and they don't know. Most people out there do not even know what they want in this life. I know an individual who had offered about seven different courses in college which did not even have any connection with each other in her life, and was still jobless. When asked why, she told me that she changed a course when she hears that another one is good. Just like this lady, most people out there do not even know what they want in this life. They move from one thing to another at the slightest change of events or challenge.

There are others too I have encountered who want to be just anything or everything. Ask them today and they will tell you that they want to be doctors. Ask them again and they want to be lawyers the next time. These people keep changing what they want until they finally become nothing at all. If you don't know what you want in this life, then you are not truly living. You're just existing and not living. Everyone was made for something. Discover who you are and what you were made to be; deciding to become it and live for that. Never allow anything to change your course and you are sure to get your way through to the top. Concentrate all your thoughts, ideas, energy, effort and resources into your dream and you will realize it. Stop doing too many things at the same time and focus on what is vital and important.

There is a man I personally know who lost a fortune, and encountered serious debt, all because he didn't learn to focus on one thing. He had started three different businesses at the same time, and by the time he realized all three were gone. I don't mean to say it is wrong to own many businesses. I actually know people out there who own different groups of companies. But the truth is that, these individuals began with one, gave it their all and made it stronger and flourishing, after which the others followed. Don't try doing many things at the same time. Start with one, especially, the one you actually love doing, give it everything you have, concentrate your effort on that one until you get the results you desire. Stop chasing two things at the same time.

It is said that if you chase two rabbits at the same time both will escape. Remember that no matter how good you are, you cannot ride two horses at the same time. You can learn many things but please specialize in something. A specialist is someone who in spite of everything he could have done, chose to focus on one. And this brings him more blessings than the one whose attention is given to everything. A normal doctor deals with the general anatomy of the body but a specialist focuses on just one part or organ of the body. A focused action is more rewarding than a divergent action. That is why it is more expensive to see a specialist. Yes, it is true that you can do all things, but you cannot do everything at the same time. To get your dream or purpose going you have to learn to focus and concentrate your energy on your definite and chief purpose. This is one of the surest ways to make it happen. If your purpose is to be a successful doctor, minister of the gospel or own your own business, just focus on it, directing and concentrating all your efforts, energy and resources towards it, and it will come to pass. Emerson said, "Concentration is the secret of strengths in politics, in war, in trade, in short; in all management of human affairs."

Andrew Carnegie had this to say, "Here is the prime condition of success: Concentrate your energy, thought and capital exclusively upon the business in which you are engaged. Having begun on one line, resolve to fight it out on that line, to lead in it, adopt every improvement, have the best machinery, and know the most about it."

"You are more likely to acquire power by narrowing your focus and applying your energies, like the sun's rays, to a limited range of activities in a small number of domains." Jeffrey Pfeiffer,

Jesus Christ also said, "No man, having put his hand to the plough, and looking back, is fit for the kingdom of God." (Luke 9:62)

Do not let anything take your mind, eyes or attention off the goal set before you. You are destined to make it like those who took the lead before you. Never forget that God wants to take you to an expected end. All you need to do is to just focus on what you are doing and do it well. Paul refused to be distracted by those things that were behind. His focus was on what was ahead. If you really have a goal to achieve, let the past be. Focus and you shall definitely be blessed.

Have you started a business, ministry or any career in life? Are you looking to excel in that which you have started? Then give it your maximum attention and concentration, and the reward in focus will come. You are not fit for success, if you are easily distracted. Keep hitting the same place of a wall with a hammer, and you are sure to make a hole in it. But if you hit different places continuously, you will get no result. When efforts converge, they make greater impact than divergent efforts. When a laser beam is focused, or converged, its power becomes intense, and can even cut. Alexander Graham Bell, the inventor of the telephone said, "The sun's rays do not burn until brought to a focus." As a warrior in this life, do not entertain distraction. Decide on what you want, be sure about it, concentrate and then give that thing your best shots and you will definitely experience a breakthrough in your life. Brian Tracy puts it this way, "Decide upon your major definite purpose in life and then organize all your activities around it."

Do you know that the light bulb is one of the blessings of focused action? Sir Thomas Edison refused to be distracted, but focused on what he desired to achieve, and it finally worked out after persisting and trying for over thousands of times. You can learn all these lessons from his life and work. He endured so much, focused on his work till the end, he showed resilience, was disciplined and chose never to give up but to persist. He was truly a warrior in real life. This can also be said of almost all the great inventors and discoverers in any field this life produced. Their inventions and discoveries were all rewards of great focus action.

They were not men who changed what they were doing because it was not working. Instead, they stuck to what they were doing, and their efforts were blessed. Don't divert from the true course because things are not happening the way you expected. Look, you cannot be an achiever if you are easily distracted. You may face challenges and very trying times. Things could look rough and very difficult. Just give it your maximum concentration, and you will achieve success in what you are pursuing. Again, do not invest your effort into doing many things at the same time. Concentrate your effort at one thing, and you will go very far with it.

3.   *Discipline*

"*All things are lawful unto me, but not all things are expedient: all things are lawful for me but I will not be brought under the power of any.*" (1 Corinthians 6: 12)

The International Standard Version of the Bible puts the above verse of scripture this way, "*Everything is permissible for me, but not everything is helpful. Everything is permissible for me, but I will not allow anything to control me.*"

There are two aspects of this; to control and to be controlled. The one who is controlled by just anything in this life will not go far. This is the attitude of those who wander in life; anything controls them. Being in control is not same as being controlled. To be able to make impact, we need to grow past that. When anything controls you, you are indiscipline. To rule our world, we need to learn to control ourselves and not allow self to control us. If you can't control yourself, you can't control people or those around you.

Most people are frustrated and depressed today because they have lived all their lives being controlled by their senses. They are controlled by their sight, instead of controlling their sight. They are controlled by taste instead of controlling their taste. They are controlled by their emotions instead of controlling their emotions, and lastly, they are controlled by what they hear instead of controlling what they hear. Successful people have all their lives learnt to master these senses whiles failures have been mastered by these senses. The art of discipline is one of the greatest virtues which ensures victory. It is true that you now have liberty to do what you want in Christ but you are advised to use your liberty well. Everything might be permissible for you but not everything will help you. Some things might be permissible for you but can damage you and your dream if you try them.

Do not be controlled by bad acts, instead, allow good acts to control you and then control the bad ones. I have said it time and time again that all sinful people are indiscipline people, who are controlled by their flesh. Control your flesh and make it live by your dictates, and not you by its dictates. You can eat everything you want but please don't just eat anything. Eat what will promote your health and not what can destroy your health. Eat to live, don't live to eat. The word which is translated expedient or helpful also means profitable. So, I think the big question you need to ask yourself is whether your choice of actions, deeds, words or moves will be profitable to what you want to achieve.

Will your actions be profitable to you? If yes then go ahead, but if not please don't try it. Hear me; you need to be disciplined to be an achiever. True success is actually the reward of great act of discipline. You cannot do anything you want and think of succeeding. There are actions which produce success. That is what you have to learn to follow if you want to succeed. Discipline was derived from the Latin word "disciplina" a word rooted to the Latin word "discipulus". The word means "pupil or disciple". That means discipline has its root from the word disciple (follower).

In other words, to be discipline is to follow a particular order of behavior or habits which ensures the production of an intended results. Any result is achievable in life. You can rise from nowhere to somewhere, from the bottom to the top, from grass to grace, from zero to billions or from shame to fame. All you need to do is to cultivate all the required habits that will ensure your intended result, and it takes discipline to do that. First of all, ask yourself, what one or set of habits do you require in order to achieve success in your respective field.

And then control yourself to follow after that until you can do those chosen habits with ease. Nothing just happens in life until somebody decides to make things happen. Don't sit and watch your life, business or ministry sink or go down the drain. Ask yourself what you are not doing right, and then make changes. As I write this book, there are things happening around me that are very tempting but I know I have to finish this manuscript for the print work to commence immediately. I thus need to restrain myself from all the temptations around in order to achieve this at the set time.

There is an attitude or behavior that produces success and there is the other which does not. A disciplined man develops that behavior that produces success by giving himself to the set of trainings which can help him develop. What you are following will determine what will follow you. Goodness and mercy will follow those who follow goodness and mercy. Set yourself to follow that which is good for you. Outline some of the things you believe can take you to your destination, and follow them strictly until you achieve what you want.

According to the opening scripture on this subject, you can do anything you want according to the law of grace, but it is not all legal things that are profitable. Most legal things will easily land you into poverty or trouble. You can sleep throughout the whole twenty-four hours given to mankind and no one will arrest you for sleeping. You can also eat or drink anything you want, while at the same time do anything you want to, and no one will hold you responsible for anything. But at the end of the day, don't complain about what you get in life. Learn to control yourself if you are an aspirant of success. Draw limits to your deeds and don't exceed those limits.

Five areas that can ensure you get a good life if properly controlled

Words

Draw limits to your words, actions, decisions and even relationships. The words you speak have power to produce the effect you want in your life. The Bible says the power of life and death is in the tongue. What you say in any given situation matters so much because it can determine the outcome of that situation. In the book of Joel 3:10, a weak person is admonished to speak strength. In other words, don't speak your situation, instead, say what you desire. If you are sick say healthy words. Like I tell people it is better to be silent than to say the wrong things. Freedom of speech has really helped the political world yet it has not done much for the individual life. You are free to say what you want but you need to be careful of what you say. If you want to excel train yourself to say the right things. Speak thoughtfully. Consider your words before you speak them. The Bible says that David was prudent in speech – meaning that he was cautious with his choice of words. Learn to speak words which bless, comfort, exhort, inspire and edify people. The Bible says, if anyone desires life and seeks good, such individual should learn to control his or her tongue (Psalm 34: 12, 13). What you say is very important in life because your words can create whatever effect you want in life. Speak life and blessings but refrain from speaking curses.

Relationship

Choose to also do only what is beneficial to your course. Shun unprofitable decisions and build good relationships with people. You can be everyone's friend but don't be a friend to everyone. It is wise to choose the people you flow with, with caution. 1 Corinthians 15:33 admonishes that bad company can corrupt any individual. It is said that your company will determine what will accompany you. If that is the case, then you need the right company to get the right results in whatever you are doing. Therefore, choose your friends and associations. If you associate with winners, you will win too. Jesus had many disciples but he chose only twelve to be close.

Determine who should be in your company and it will benefit you at the end. Be nice to everyone but please understand that not all people can be your friends. Proverbs 13:20 say, by walking with the wise, you shall be wise. If so, just think about what walking with the right people will do for you. Be in the company of those who can inspire and encourage you to be a better person. There are people who don't add anything to you when you keep their company. It is better to shun such company if you are aspiring to succeed.

Time

One of the awesome gifts of life is time. God lives beyond time but then He gave us time. We know that one day time will end which the Bible calls end time but now we are still here in time. After God created heaven and earth, the next thing he worked on was time (day and night). Genesis 1:5 says and the evening and the morning was the first day. As much as time is a gift from the Creator, how we use it determines what we get from it. If you will enjoy life, you will have to learn to use your time properly. Manage your time well and you shall be rewarded. Outline your lists of activities within the 24 hours that you have. Make changes or adjustments where necessary and then carry on with the beneficial things you do.

Remember if you spend your time watching movies or television, don't expect success. Invest time in profitable things that will add value to you and not things that will waste you out. If you have discovered your purpose or definite aim, then use all the time that you have at your disposal to make it work by investing it into all the appropriate things you need to do to achieve your dream. Please understand that you can't eat your cake and have it. Time wasted cannot be regained, so you need to be cautious with how you use your time. One of the differences between successful men and the unsuccessful is what they use their time for. Successful men use their time improving themselves whiles the unsuccessful engages in unbeneficial things.

Finance

This is one area in life I guess everyone should handle well. Nobody wants to be poor in life. We all want to be financially free, though not all are free financially. This is because it is not automatic to be financially free. Great measure of discipline is required to be able to achieve that. Every one of us needs to learn self-control in the area of spending. Financially free people exercise great prudence in how they use their money. They don't just buy anything, they purchase useful things. If you want to be financially free reduce consumption and increase your investments.

Spend money on assets and not liabilities. Buy what you need and not what you want. This is a very important virtue to develop. How most people think when they don't have money is different from how they think when they get money in hand. Never let money control you when it starts coming, learn to control it. Build proper financial plan for yourself and follow it till you achieve your financial dream. You can also seek professional advice here, and then follow strictly what you learn till your dream is achieved.

Food

Eat to live, don't live to eat. This is a very important statement in building a healthy life. Significantly, every human need a healthy life to go about their normal daily activities. Diseases or sicknesses are considered to be one of the greatest tragedies humanity is plagued with. And most of the diseases and disabilities are caused by unhealthy eating. Diseases like high blood pressure, obesity, diabetes, heart disease, cancer and even stroke stem from unhealthy dieting. Please do not be controlled by your tongue, you need to control it rather. Eat the right types of food and also don't eat late. Prevent any of the above diseases by making the right choices of food. Learn to control your senses and this will be easy for you.

Emotions

It is said that great men control their emotions and are not controlled by their emotions. Many individuals have missed great deals because their actions were emotionally driven. Isaac passed on his blessing to Jacob instead of Esau because he chose to follow his feeling. Many people have been led astray into taking wrong decisions and moves because they chose to follow their feelings. Don't be in a rush to take actions when you feel angry, jealous, or sad, and even in happy moods. This does not mean that emotions are always bad. All I want you to understand is that they shouldn't be your base for making judgments.

Discipline is significant if you can make progress in any field of endeavor. George Washington said, "*Discipline is the soul of an army. It makes small numbers formidable; procures success to the weak, and esteem to all.*" A weak man who is disciplined is better than a strong man who is indiscipline. Please understand that you can't afford to be careless with your actions and make progress to your dream goal at the same time. You need to know what to do and what not to do to get to that goal. Success has never been by accident. One needs to desire and pursue it to have it. There are actions you do that will lead you to your dream goal.

Discover those actions and pursue them strictly until you get what you want. Discipline, is knowing those things you must do and those you must not do and following them to the latter. If you see one man rise over his fellows in the same field of endeavor, the difference might probably be in what he is doing right the others are not doing or what he is not doing the others are doing. Discipline always gives a man an edge over another, whether in business, football, the Lord's vineyard or in any field of endeavor. George Washington is again quoted, *"Nothing is more harmful to the service, than the neglect of discipline; for that discipline, more than numbers give army superiority over another."*

The man who has learnt to conquer himself can conquer anything. Learn to control yourself, and you can control anything. To be an effective leader, you need to learn how to lead or direct yourself. To master the world, master yourself, and others will follow. If you can restrain yourself from doing what is irrelevant to victory and success, then you will find yourself on the brink of victory. There are many things that have formed habits in us, and are very perilous to progress which can be changed on the altar of discipline. In order to succeed, how you spend your time and resources are very important. The poor man has the same 24hrs as the rich man, but the difference between the two is what they do in this 24hrs, and this includes what they spend their time thinking about, reading and watching. All great men are men of disciplined acts.

Great men and women live very narrow and orderly lives. Their time is divided evenly throughout the whole-time frame of the day, doing what shall be profitable to their course. They eat what shall make them healthy for their course. They are not emotionally driven, but whatever they do, they do because it is relevant to the attainment of their goal. But poor people do the contrary. There were individuals who inherited great wealth and possessions but came to nothing due to their habits of indiscipline.

Do you remember the story of the prodigal son in the Bible? I call it the story of the indiscipline son. After getting all he needed from his father, he travelled to a far away country and squandered everything he gained on unprofitable living, and at the end returned with nothing in hand. No matter what you have, if you are indiscipline, you are in danger. It is better to be disciplined and have no material possessions now than to have every material possession but is indiscipline. History is full of entrepreneurs, athletes, preachers and other professionals who easily lost all their fortunes and goodwill to indiscipline.

The problem with the prodigal son was not, what he didn't have, but his way of life. Indiscipline is the reason why most people who gain wealth through inheritance lose everything in a short time. Just as there are stories of men who have ascended up the ladder of success due to their level of discipline, there are also men who have descended that same ladder due to indiscipline. I once read about a young man who rose to fame and became one of the greatest and skillful footballers the world has ever produced, but he sadly lost his place because he lost the art of discipline which ensured that he become distinct and rose to the top.

Instead of training and improving, he shunned training sessions and became a regular night club attendant doing unnecessary things all the time. This began to affect his performances until he lost his place to another who became better through the art of discipline. It is true that discipline is not sweet but it is very rewarding. The Bible says, *"No discipline seems pleasant at the time, but painful. Later on, however, it produces a harvest of righteousness and peace for those who have been trained by it."* Hebrews (12: 11, ISV).

I know that you are reading this book because you have a desire to succeed. Continue doing the right things. Do not use your liberty wrongly. Choose and decide on things that will be profitable to you and your dream. If you are a minister of the gospel, note that your success in ministry also hinges around discipline. It takes a great act of discipline to pray and study for long hours. It even takes discipline to wait on God. I believe where the Bible says, "they that wait upon the Lord" refers to those who could exercise enough discipline to see the Lord move on their behalf. This is because it takes great act of discipline to wait on the Lord. As much as independence is good, one of its challenges is indiscipline. Since people can think, say and do what they like, they take this into their personal lives, thus hindering success or progress. You cannot do just anything and be successful. You need to put yourself under some set of rules or obligations to get yourself going. This answers the reason why every institution has rules they work with, which to the institution ensures success. You are bound for success, so do not waste your time and resources on unbeneficial things. Program yourself for success and you will succeed.

4. *Resilience*

The fourth ability or virtue of the soldier that is relevant to success or victory in this life is resilience. This is the ability to recover fully from adversity, stress, disappointment or losses. Have you noticed how elastic recovers after being stretched? That is exactly what I mean here. As a good soldier you need to learn how to recover from shock, depression, stress, defeat or even failure when this life begins stretching you, because it will. As you journey the road that leads to your destiny, there are surely going to be temporary defeats. There are also times that you may feel discouraged, disappointed or broken.

There are people going through diverse kinds of issues which may have in turn hijacked their performances or destinies. There are people suffering from pains of the past, bitterness, broken heart, losses, setbacks, failure, and disappointment not because it should have, but then they gave in and threw down the towel when faced with these challenging issues. I know people who opted for suicide after they lost all hope of making progress or surviving in this life. I have encountered men and women who have lost the desire for marriage or relationship due to emotional injuries and wounds they suffered from past relationships.

I know a preacher who gave up his work after the loss of his wife having gone through emotional disappointments, stress and depression. Life is full of people who are despaired and have given up living due to one issue or the other. There are several others who have been victimized and bound by certain perplexing situations.

One of the things I want you to understand is that every individual goes through one of these challenges or troubles in life. The difference is not about what we go through but how we treat what we go through. This is also the difference between successful people and those who do not succeed. Successful people go through the same challenges or troubles as everybody, but what they do differently is; they do not allow the things they go through to bind, define or hold them back. They encourage and gird themselves up despite the pains from past injuries, wounds, defeats, mistakes and then move on, while the others get stacked at one place by the things they go through. Hear me; do not let your past hold you.

You might have committed strange mistakes in life or done something wrong, but you shouldn't allow these to hold you back from doing what you ought to do to progress. Understand that these things are normal. You may have encountered very discouraging and disappointing things in life. There were times that I even wanted to take my own life due to some of the things I was going through but then my perspective changed. My dear, this is reality. Stop crying over that loss in your life and move on. I know it is not easy, but should you let that hold you back. Everybody knows that you have made a mistake, but shouldn't you correct yourselves and move on. Do not wear yourself out because you feel that you messed up badly.

Have you ever heard of the phrase "to err is human?" this means that as much as we are still humans and still in this house called 'body,' mistakes will still happen. There are times that we would feel defeated, whipped or brutalized. There are also times that we would encounter hurts, pains, wounds or heartbreaks as we journey the path of destiny. But should we allow these happenings to change us and give us a negative orrientation towards life. Please no! Hold your peace, keep your cool, make amends and move on. Do not allow your past or present mistakes or wounds to imprison you. There is a whole land of beauty and glory ahead of you. Ignore those men who make facing challenges seem so abnormal. Life is neither a plateau nor a smooth course. It is also never free of challenges or problems.

I do not dispute the fact that Christ died and rose for us, but that was not to change this world and its systems. He died and rose to change us for a better living here and in the hereafter. His death and resurrection did not change the events of life, meaning that, we still face some of the things this world faces. Christ's death and resurrection did not bring an end to challenges; rather it produced a new creation. A new breed of man who goes through what everyone goes through but differently. The truth is that the same storm that blows against unbelievers blows against the believer. But in our case, we have what it takes to sail through any circumstance or issue unharmed and unraffled. Never forget that in the book of Matthew 7: 25, Jesus spoke about some floods, and winds that come to test our foundation. That is what I am talking about. There is no place in the Bible, where God promised an easy ride or smooth road to our destiny.

I believe in the finished work of Christ. I know and am aware of what God has done for us in Christ Jesus. I also believe in the new creation reality and the abilities of the new creation man. I know God's greatest investment was in the new creation man and that the new creation has all the virtues he needs to make life in his spirit or nature. But it all depends on us to build and develop these virtues of which resilience is one of them. You need this ability to survive anytime you are stretched. Forgive and forget those wrongs and pains people have caused you so that you can gain your peace and life back. Do not let bitterness and hatred block the flow of good things in you. Learn to forgive and ignore offences so that you can move on.

Forget about what you have lost for there are better things ahead of you. You need to make life and fulfill your dreams. Cease worrying about your past defeats and focus on the success ahead. No matter how down you are, you can get back on your feet again – be encouraged. You can recover from any fall if only you will give yourself the chance. Do you know that one of the things Christianity came to show us through its message of resurrection is that there is no hopeless situation? No problem is too big to solve. Jesus clearly showed that by raising the dead. According to John 10:10, His mission statement is to give life in abundance, and He proved this to Martha, the sister of Mary and Lazarus, that He is the resurrection and life by raising Lazarus from the dead. You can recover from any fall, defeat or pain. What makes a righteous man unique is his ability to rise when he falls. The Bible says though he falls seven times, he shall rise again (Proverbs 24:16).

Being able to recover after a major crisis is very vital in every story of success. In his book, "The Assignment," Dr. Mike Murdock underwrites, "Crisis is a normal event on the road to your assignment." Your ability to recover from shock, disappointments, defeat or from a fall matters a lot. It will interest you to know that many lives, visions, ideas and discoveries have been terminated all due to the inability of the person involved to recover from defeats, pain, disappointment or depression. If you do not learn to overcome the hurts, pain and disappointments that you go through, you will remain stacked. There are people who cannot trust anybody due to betrayals and disappointments from people who were close.

Do you know that most of the people in most of our mental asylums are individuals who are suffering from emotional and psychological traumas? Over the past decade in ministry, I have come across pastors who withdrew from the service of God owing to unexpected or heartbreaking mistakes they made. But then there are some also who rebounded quickly even from the most tragic and shocking experiences they encountered in life. Please understand that, life does not end when you encounter injuries or wounds. You might have suffered from something strange either from a disease or an amputation of your feet or arm, I encourage you not to give up on yourself yet. Life does not end with the end of an arm or limb. Do not be broken or shattered. Understand that your progress or success in life is not limited to that.

Let the story of Helen Keller, the first deaf, blind and dumb woman to obtain a bachelors' degree in arts inspire you, if you were born with any challenge or birth defect. There is also the story of Thomas Edison and the others to encourage you, if you feel defeated, deteriorated and discouraged and are on the verge of giving up. All you need to do is to believe that this life is not over for you. Encourage yourself and then journey on. God has very wonderful plans for you, so pull yourself together and begin to consider what He has placed ahead for you, and you will definitely do wonders. The ability to get back up or rebound after any major crisis is one of the most precious virtues everybody will need to reach his or her goal.

One day, David and his army returned from a mission to only realize that all they had worked for in their entire lives were gone, including their wives and children. The Bible says that David's men wept till they had no more power to weep. This tells you how ruined they felt they were after discovering their houses burnt, with family and property all gone. But David didn't give up or kill himself. Instead the Bible says that he encouraged himself, pursued the enemies with some of his men after enquiring from God and then they recovered everything they had lost. Until you recover, you cannot deliver. Everyone is aware that adversity is not a nice experience, yet if you won't get discouraged and broken because of what you are going through, but will pull yourself together, encourage yourself and carry on, you are surely going to win. Do not let anything stop you from pursuing your dream, whether hurts, pains, shock, depression, frustration or even disappointment. Press on till you get to your intended destination. You can achieve your dream; no matter your current situation, so don't give up or retire. Who told you that you are finished because you lost what you have? Who told you your end has come? Stop blaming yourself for what went wrong in the past, and look ahead. Let those things that are destroyed be. There is nothing you cannot achieve. There are better things ahead. There are great opportunities and blessings ahead so please don't harm or kill yourself for what you lost. Let what is gone be gone and focus on what is ahead. You might have lost someone you love, something you cherish, a fortune, or even lost everything.

I once read the story of a man who lost a fortune to fire. Everything he had worked for throughout his life time was gone, and one would think that he was going to be shattered or frustrated, but instead he demonstrated a great act of courage and faith, despite what had happened. His own words sum it all, "As a human, I became troubled and very devastated when the news got to me, but on a second thought I realized that I only lost a fortune, and not what produced that fortune. So I pulled myself together to continue living." This man indeed made great progress when he decided to let go the past and focus on what was ahead after he recovered from that shock.

Do not be discouraged, it is not yet over. Pull yourself together, and then forge on to victory, and all shall be well. Don't remain on the ground of battle. Yea, you fell but get back up. I hear someone say, "You don't understand. I have committed a grievous crime and I don't think I will ever be pardoned." Hear me; do not let your thoughts ruin you. The problem is not in what you have done but in what you are thinking. God is never condemning you for what you have done. You will only be condemned for not accepting His means of forgiveness. He says, "Though your sins be as scarlet, they shall be white as snow; though they be red like crimson, they shall be like wool" Isaiah 1: 18. Stop living in guilt, forgive yourself because God is not holding any grudge against you, correct yourself, forget the past and move on.

Perseverance

There is a story in the book of Luke 18:3-5 about a certain importunate widow who demanded justice of a judge from her adversaries and things she suffered. This is good example of what persistent efforts can achieve. It clearly indicates that God honors persistent efforts. The wicked judge always ignored this widow, until he one day became fed up with the continual pestering of this woman. I believe that story is not just coincidentally shared in the scriptures but a purposeful illustration by Jesus showing us how much we can achieve if we persevere in any pursuit. Perseverance is a very great key to success, and it is that character or quality that urges an individual to continue doing something even though it is difficult. Perseverance makes you insist on your pursuit or remain constant to a purpose, idea or task in the face of obstacles, discouragement, warnings, setbacks or problem. It also means being tenacious. You can do all you know to do to succeed, but without perseverance you have almost no chance of success. This is one of the closest to success, if not the closest. A friend once said perseverance is the last sign post to success. In other words when you get to that point in your life or pursuit where you are required to hold on and keep pressing to be able to progress, amidst obstacles, challenges setbacks or difficulties, it means that you are very close to success. Wherever and whenever a man persists nobody can dismantle the flag of success. One hidden truth I believe all must be aware of is that, as a person gets closer to victory in their pursuit, the journey gets tougher, painful and uncomfortable. The Bible says in the book of John 16:21 (NRSV) that, "**When a woman is in labor she has pain, because her hour has come. But when her child is born, she no longer remembers the anguish because of the joy of having brought a human being into the world.**" Labor is when a woman enters her due season of delivery, and the

Bible confirms that things get rough in these times of delivery. It always gets painful when you are close to the victory, yet it does not mean that you should stop pursuing your dream or give up on it.

What is expected of you is to keep your composure and press on till you achieve the results you desire. If you persist in your pursuit refusing to give up, you will surely get to the victory. Roger Bannister said, *"The man who can drive himself further once the effort gets painful is the man who will win."* Do not give up yet. You are too close to give up. Most times, the distance between where people give up and the place of success is a very short one. A wise man once said, *"Most people give up just when they are about to achieve success. They quit on the one-yard line. They give up at the last minute of the game, one foot from a winning touchdown."* This is what has happened to many people in life. They gave up when they were so close to winning. A little push or effort would have taken them through but they become overwhelmed by the challenges they face and then they give up.

Just get your eyes fixed on the prize or victory, never allowing anything to discourage you from advancing or progressing to the end. This is exactly what David did when he encountered Goliath as he visited his brethren on the battlefield. 1 Samuel 17:26 says, "And David spake to the men that stood by him, saying, what shall be done to the man that killeth this Philistine, and taketh away the reproach from Israel? For who *[is]* this uncircumcised Philistine, that he should defy the armies of the living God?" You see, as much as David was concerned Goliath was not a problem at all provided the reward was good. And when he realized how good the prize was, he did not allow anyone to discourage him, including his brethren and King Saul.

If you quit because things are getting tougher, then you are robbing yourself a great opportunity to become a champion. Quitters indeed never win, whereas winners never quit. Winners keep at what they are doing no matter the challenges, frustrations, obstacles or difficulties.

They do not stop until they get to their intended destinations or get their desired results. Persistence is an important virtue if anyone will succeed. Emerson said, *"The characteristic of genuine heroism is its persistency."*

Calvin Coolidge, the 30th president of the United States also said, *"Persistence and determination alone are omnipotent. The slogan press on has solved and always will solve the problems of the human race."*

B. C. Forbes said, *"History has demonstrated that the most notable winners usually encountered heartbreaking obstacles before they triumphed. They won because they refused to become discouraged by their defeats."*

Mario Andretti said, *"Desire is the key to motivation, but it is determination and commitment to an unrelenting pursuit of your goal - a commitment to excellence - that will enable you to attain the success you seek."*

Tommy Lasorda said, *"The difference between the impossible and the possible lies in a man's determination."*

Keep going, though it is not easy. For the word 'difficulty' does not mean impossible. All it means is that you need to push and work hard. Continue pressing until you get the breakthrough. A little more energy and effort could have taken you there, had you not given up so soon. How sad it is when many a times people give up when they are so close to the victory. Norman Vincent Peale said, *"It is always too soon to quit."* Keep pushing, do not get discouraged and it will happen. Persistent action is always rewarding. Don't give up on what you are doing, and you will surely make a mark. Persistence is one of the most important things you need on your way to fulfilling destiny. The book of James 5:17-18 shows that it was Elijah's persistency in prayer that stopped the rains and also brought it back.

He was tenacious and very insistent in his request that he was not ready to give up praying, even when there was no sign of success.

He kept at it until he achieved the results he was looking for. The verse 17 of the chapter says, ***"Elijah was a man to like passions as we are, but he prayed earnestly."*** In other words, Elijah could have given up like any ordinary person would. He had feelings just like you and I. He could be disappointed and even frustrated like us all. But his persistency in prayer was what got him going this time when everything seemed failing. Persistence is the difference between those who achieve success and those who do not. Vince Lombardi said, *"The difference between a successful person and others is not a lack of strength, not a lack of knowledge, but rather a lack of determination."*

I once heard the story of a man who missed a great deal of wealth because of his impatience. He was told of a land full of gold and other precious gems. Upon hearing this, he went to purchase that land, but after digging several feet down and seeing no gold, he became discouraged. Later he decided to dig some additional feet to see whether he would discover the gold, but unfortunately he still didn't find any. On the third time, he decided to continue digging a little more, after which he would pack his equipment and leave if he did not see any good sign. This time round he discovered a very big, but hard rock.

After digging a feet of the rock and seeing no positive sign, he dropped his tool in despair, came to pack his equipment and left. Many years later, another man also came to purchase that same piece of land. This man dug through until he also got to that same big rock. When he got to the rock, he saw an old, rusted pickaxe in the rock. He then realized that somebody had dug that piece of land before. This time, this man continued to dig through that hard rock, and to his surprise, after just digging two feet from where he found the pickaxe, he saw what he had not seen before. He finally met the treasure he was seeking. Would you continue pressing until something happens? Your treasure awaits you!

Chapter 4

DEVELOP A PRUDENT APPROACH

*"... **and prudent in matters** ..."* (1Samuel 16:18)

This is another important quality relevant for a successful advancement to any glorious destination. Remember that, every quality being discussed in all the chapters is a very important recipe for a successful journey towards destiny. Knowing that you already understand what destiny is, right from the beginning of this journey, I want to add that, the fulfillment of one's destiny is one of the glorious achievements of living. I believe that if everybody should be who God destined he or she to be, this world will know enough peace, and would be better than it is. I believe that the best thing an individual can be is to be him or herself. This is one of the greatest blessings humanity would have enjoyed, but have missed because few individuals ever achieved this. And this is so because, being your true self requires a great deal of development which includes all that is being discussed in this book.

The reason why people run away from partaking in the story of destiny is that it takes great strength to reach there and all these qualities which each chapter talks about combined is what I call STRENGTH. No person ever attained any greater height in this life without these qualities, and one of them is PRUDENCE. Prudence is the quality of approaching situations thoughtfully, considering the possibilities and risk at play. It also means taking time to assimilate context and history prior to launching into action. It means reality-checking our own assumptions and instinctual reactions. A prudent man or woman takes a wise approach in handling practical matters; that is, he exercises good judgment or common sense in handling issues. Being prudent is taking caution in managing one's activities or resources.

The Bible clearly emphasized that this was one of David's qualities that got him a place in the palace where he actually belonged. One version puts the above verse this way, "he is an able speaker." In other words he exercised great caution at speaking. He didn't just speak anything he liked, rather he spoke what was relevant, and he was noted for this. Even at the age of sixteen, David was noted for exhibiting a great skill in speech management. And this was worthy of a King. It is a kingly attribute. He spoke what would bless, exhort and change. Though he had not become a king yet, he possessed a kingly attribute. You may not be a physical king, but a king in business, ministry, music, medicine, law and many more. And you will have to understand that prudence is one of the qualities you would need to get to your destiny. That is being discreet and cautious at managing your activities and resources so as to get an intended result. Success does not just happen, and it is not just any action that produces a needed result.

Success or progress requires taking very wise, calculated actions. You have to learn to advance by approaching issues thoughtfully. By considering the possibilities and risk at play before we dare out, we are able to proceed with greater clarity and confidence. This often prevents nasty mistakes and unnecessary detours by reminding us to listen and learn. A wise man once said, "*Caution is not cowardice. Carelessness is not courage.*" Making careless actions can cost you more than you thought. It pays to be cautious. And never forget that being cautious does not mean you are afraid, it rather means you are learning to take wise actions that will produce results at the end.

Prudence lets you study what is ahead and what the journey is made up of, so that you can prepare before daring out. Risk becomes manageable if you already know what is at stake or prepared for the unexpected, but the ignorance of what lies ahead can bring much shock and pain than anticipated. Esther didn't approach King Ahasuerus as an ignorant person; she knew what was at stake. She was aware that she could lose her life in the process and at the same time she was aware that favor could be done her, if the King holds out his golden scepter to her. This helped her to know the right actions to take for the breakthrough to happen, and indeed it did happen.

The ancient nations were used to sending people to spy on a land before they attacked it. This was to help them strategize and draw proper plan for attacking on the premise of very relevant information. Spies are tasked with ensuring that enough information are gathered about the land a people intended to capture. They try to find out both the strength and weakness of their enemies before they launch out to fight with them. An example of this is in the book of Joshua 2: 1-24. Great and successful men are not only action takers; they learn to take the right action at the right time. This is very important if any individual wants to make a mark in this life.

God does not want you to take just an action, He wants you to take an analytical look at the situation, know and understand what is involved before you make a move. If you don't have any idea or knowledge about what you want to do, seek counsel somewhere, especially from those who have excelled in your field of endeavor. Prudence will not just make a farm or cultivate anything at any time but will study and analyze seasons before. It will seek to know which crop type survives in each season. It studies the conditions needed for any crop before it invests into that. It is better to run your life or vision on a relevant information. When you know what is ahead, you act with confidence.

Prudence says, wait, don't go yet, instead seek what you need to know before you dare out. One man said, *"The man who knows when not to act is wise. To my mind, bravery is forethought."*

Jesus taught a great lesson in Luke 14:28-32, on prudence when He advised that we count the cost before making a move. This is to save us from making any unbearable mistake. Yes, it is true that the road that leads to your destiny is not an easy one, but it becomes more perilous if you don't act with prudence. There is one particular tribe among the twelve tribes of Israel, called Issachar, who were men known for their understanding of the times, to know when Israel ought to do anything.

And of the children of Issachar, [which were men] that had understanding of the times, to know what Israel ought to do ... 1 Chronicles 12: 32.

That is a great gift of attitude, because it always prevents mistakes. I believe these men who had these great understanding of the times Israel ought to do anything were men who studied, analyzed and planned before giving any instruction to move. And you know, this would prevent any mistake and silly moves. This is why prudence is important. Many people are stacked in the way because, they didn't count the cost involve so that they could lay down a good plan that would lead them to their intended dream. They just launch out without any good plan and as a result are sabotaged by their own carelessness. Don't be in a haste to get anywhere. Be wise, take your time and be led. The Bible says, *"He that hasteth to be rich [hath] an evil eye, and considereth not that poverty shall come upon him"* (Proverbs 28: 22).

Be wise by analyzing and planning before you dare out. There are people out there who could have done better by being prudent before daring out, but dared out without being cautious and not carefully planning. Don't just make any investment because you like investing or because you were told. As much as investment is good you need to make wise investments. You need to study and analyze the trend of market with regards to what you are investing in before taking action. Many people have lost a fortune due to the lack of taking very analytical and cautious step before making any decision. A lot more have also lost their lives because of this same thing.

I believe that the reason why Jesus told His disciples to tarry until they were filled with power from on high is that, after taking an analytical look at the nature of the work, He noticed it couldn't be done without the help of the power of God. Prudence helps you prepare efficiently for the battle. Being prudent does not mean that an individual fears, but instead that individual is being cautious. Max Lucado Pastor of Oak Hill Church said, *"The step between prudence and paranoia is short and steep. Prudence wears a seat belt. Paranoia avoids cars. Prudence washes with soap. Paranoia avoids human contact. Prudence saves for old age. Paranoia hoards even trash. Prudence prepares and plans, paranoia panics. Prudence calculates the risk and takes the plunge. Paranoia never enters the water."*

One day I entered a village with about two friends for visitation, and before we got to our destination, we came across a small stream with no bridge. And we had to cross this stream before we could get to our destination. Since we were in a haste to reach our destination on time, without any delay, I tried stepping into the river. But before I could step into it, one of the friends screamed, 'wait'. So I stopped moving, and then asked to know why he ordered me to stop. And before I could ask why, he picked a long stick from a nearby bush and dipped it into the water to check its depth. After checking where I wanted to step, he checked some other places and then beckoned us to follow him.

Though we mocked, calling him experienced village man, I pondered quietly on the whole scene whiles we journeyed on, and wondered what could have happened without that piece of wisdom from that friend. Hear me; to act without wisdom is very perilous. We were all saved that day by that prudent act of the friend. Was what my friend did fear? No! It was caution instead. This is what is called prudence. Prudence ensures safety, and prevents harm. My friend's action that day saved us from a possible harm and thought me a great lesson. Do not jump into taking any unanalyzed action. As much as daring out is good always take caution to know what is involved before you dare out.

Characteristics of a prudent man

He acts with wisdom

The wise in heart shall be called prudent: and the sweetness lips increaseth learning (Proverbs 16: 21).

It is impossible to be prudent without wisdom. Proverbs chapter eight verse twelve says wisdom dwells with prudence. So we can say that a prudent man is also wise man. James chapter three verse thirteen shows that wise men are known by their conversations and works or deeds. He exercises discretion, insight and good judgments in his dealing with others. He is also humble enough to accept change, instruction and even corrections from either his peers or his seniors.

He has foresight

A prudent man foreseeth … (Proverbs 27:12).

Foresight is the ability to plan for the future. And this is one of the main character traits of a prudent man. He is driven by the future. His actions in the present are driven or motivated by what he seeks to achieve in the future. That was the difference between Esau and Jacob in the Bible. Jacob's focus was the future whiles Esau's was the present. By his statement in Genesis 25: 32, we know that Esau was not considering the future but the present. A prudent man's actions in the present is inspired by their vision. He does not mind giving his all just to have the future he wants. If it even requires that he goes hungry by sacrifices his sweet pottage just like Jacob, he will do it in order to have his dream realized. He is an investor, not a consumer. He is giver and a sower.

He anticipates evil and takes initiative

A prudent man foreseeth evil and hideth himself ... (Proverbs 27:12)

One of the main nature of prudence is anticipating evil and taking initiatives to avoid it. There are some evil happenings which cannot be stopped but can be avoided and this is what prudence does. This life is full of many unexpected happenings. So as much as you plan and prepare for your expectations, also consider what you are not expecting and plan for it. A prudent man is able to look ahead and read all possible risks or dangers that lays ahead of him, and what he does afterwards is to hide himself. In other words he takes initiative which can keep him when the evils he perceives happen. When Joseph perceived by the dream of Pharaoh the famine that was ahead, he demanded for good initiatives to be taken so that they could be hidden from the famine. And that was exactly what happened.

He loves knowledge

The heart of the prudent getteth knowledge; and the ear of the wise seeketh knowledge. (Proverbs 18:15)

No human has ever lived in life with full knowledge of everything. Even the knowledgeable of all men still knows that there are still things they do not know. So we are all still ignorant in many ways. A prudent man understands and knows that there are still more to know in life and so presses for knowledge. He always keeps himself updated with current information even if it requires paying for it. They always embrace all opportunities to know more in what they are about whether in conferences, seminar and workshops or even if they have to go back to school.

Plan Before You Step Out

No battle is won without a good plan. A plan is a very important thing to success. A good plan will ensure that we enjoy the best ride on the way to our destination. Possessing a good plan can distinguish you and give you a better performance in any field in this life. An unplanned life is an undirected life. A good plan fetches a good price. Without a plan, you will wander. Great men always plan and prepares before they launch out. The best things in life always become the portion of good planners. Planning is the greatest part of any preparation process before action is made. It is planning that explains how the journey to your destination might be, what you need to make that journey and what to do in order to have a good journey. This makes your journey easier and safer. Every great institution is the result of good planning.

A good plan will ensure a good run. A goal without a plan is just a mere wish. How sad it is for a man to have a vision but have no plan that will lead him to achieving his dream. A dream without a plan is but a daydream. All achievers did not only have a goal, they mapped up a plan to achieve their goal. A plan shows the way and strategy being used to achieve a particular goal or aim. In football, the successes of coaches are dependent on their ability to devise good plan which is normally called 'game plan' to win their matches. Planning is very vital and relevant in any successful journey. Having a goal you want to achieve is nice, but if you lack the plan which will lead you in achieving that goal you may end up with nothing. You are free to dream big, nevertheless, the fulfillment of your dream is not automatic. You need a plan that will get you going.

The achievement of any dream or vision is possible. There is nothing you want to do in this life that you cannot do. You can rise to a level of prominence and relevance in life. If you have thought about it or imagined it, just believe that you can, and you will achieve it. You can be one of the best in your field of endeavor. You can build that dream business or ministry. You can be that champion you dream of becoming. All things are possible to him who believes. All dreams are achievable. Greatness is attainable. Success is reachable. But between where you are and where you dream to be is a big gap, and it takes good planning to get there.

Abraham Lincoln said, "*If we could first know where we are, and whither we are tending, we could better judge what to do, and how to do it.*" That is planning. Just imagine yourself given the task of climbing to the top of a tower without any stairway, elevator or even anything that can help you up to the top. Ask yourself what you are going to do to make that happen. Remember that it is possible to get that done if believe you can.

One day a group of young men were asked to watch carefully a mountain in their area that had never been climbed before due to its steepness with each of them coming up with a possible strategy that can help them get to the top of the mountain. After a while each individual was asked to show what strategy they had devised so far and it was only one of them who could impress everybody. He did not only write what he would do but sketched how the whole thing was going to be. He then came out to explain that he believed that his plan will easily help him but could take a while because it requires working on the mountain each day to make sure it becomes possible to climb.

There could have been a better way but he had decided to dig a stairway not straight to the top but around the mountain and in areas that could be dug so that climbing it would be easier. This is how it is in real life. To do the impossible, it is never enough to have just a vision. You need a plan that can take you to that destination you want to achieve. A vision will only show or inform you about the end from where you are, but you require a very strategic plan to get there. And good plan is the road map to that vision.

H. Stanley Judd is quoted to have said, *"A good plan is like a road map: it shows the final destination and usually the best way to get there."* Earl Nightingale, an American radio announcer, author and motivational speaker who lived between 1921 and 1989 also said, *"All you need is the plan, the road map, and the courage to press on to your destination."* I have come across men and women who had great ideas, dreams and visions but never achieved anything. Some people have dreamt all their lives. Would you be surprised to know that, most of the wonderful things we see and enjoy were actually the ideas and dreams of some individuals who did not have any plan to realize them.

It is said that before the Wright brothers invented the airplane, people had already thought about that and tried the idea before. The difference is that the Wright brothers didn't only think about the possibility of the airplane but thought also of a good work plan to making it happen. Achievers possess a road map to their destination. A plan is a list of actions arranged in whatever sequence is thought likely to achieve an objective. Alan Lakein said, *"Planning is bringing the future into the present so that you can do something about it now."* God himself is a great planner. He will never give any individual an assignment without a plan to get it done.

He didn't only tell Noah to build Him the ark, He gave him the plan. He also gave Moses the plan and design of the tabernacle He wanted him to build. Any time His people were faced with war or battle, He didn't just speak to them about victory, He introduced them to the plan that would get them to achieve victorious results. The book of Joshua 6 shows God's plan for defeating and conquering Jericho. There are several other passages in the Bible that show God's plan for getting a particular result achieved.

He gave King Jehoshaphat a plan for defeating the people of Moab and Ammon (2 Chronicles 20). He always has a plan for any assignment He gives His children to do. If God has given you any assignment, just wait patiently for him and He will unfold to you His plan that will help you in completing that task as you wait on Him. God is indeed a great planner, who does not execute any mission without a plan. When you read the first two chapters of the book of Genesis, you will realize that there are two different accounts on creation. Though the two chapters seem different, they are not.

The first account which is chapter one of Genesis is the plan whereas the second account is the actual creation. God planned for everything before He made them. This tells us the significance of planning in our lives. We cannot do away with it in any area of our lives. We must plan each day of our lives so that we can achieve the success we desire. Every move and step we make must be planned according to our set goals. Plan each year, month and days in your life very well. If you don't, you easily become a prey or victim to any situation in this life.

As a plan plays a great role in the construction of any building, every individual needs a good plan to build a good life. A good plan will ensure a good run. The plan shows every detail of what is going to be done and where each should be done so as to achieve the required goal. Take time to plan before stepping out to achieve your dream. Pablo Picasso said, *"Our goals can only be reached through a vehicle of a plan, in which we must fervently believe, and upon which we must vigorously act. There is no other route to success."*

Margaret Thatcher said, *"Plan your work for today and every day, then work your plan."*

Plan your life goal, using the resources at your disposal, which includes your time, money, gifts and every other tool relevant for success. Seek to know which types of actions or steps will get you going, and then follow them up strictly. French dramatist, novelist and poet, Victor Hugo, said, *"He who every morning plans the transaction of the day and follows out that plan, carries a thread that will guide him through the maze of the most busy life. But where no plan is laid, where the disposal of time is surrendered merely to the chance of incidence, chaos will soon reign."* Take time to plan every detail of your life. Plan every minute of each day in your life.

Don't let any hour go unutilized. Take hold of every moment of your life and use it for something that will take you a bit closer to your destiny each day. Every successful man has a plan he is working with. Successful men plan their days, weeks, months and years. Can you tell me what you want to achieve in the next five years and how you intend to do it, if I should ask you? That is the problem with most people. Though they want to be great and successful, they don't have any plan in making their dreams come true. Build a development plan towards achieving your goal and follow it up. Plan every detail of your life depending on your calling or your goal. If you are a minister of the gospel, make sure that your daily plans, schedules and activities are taking you further towards achieving your goal. My day as a minister of the gospel is scheduled and planned with much carefulness.

Every hour in each day is occupied with an activity of importance. No hour is allowed to go without being used for something of great benefit to my calling, mission and personal or family life. I do not only plan my day but also discipline myself to follow suit as planned. To have a plan, but lack the discipline to follow that plan makes you useless like the one who does not have a plan. The reward is in following the plan up until you achieve your goal. This is what I strive doing each day. Following my plans for the day works the wonders in my life.

I have a personal prayer time which last three hours each day, a time for studies and fellowship with the Word of God; I also have a reading time I have termed 'read a book', I have a time for visitation, meetings and attending services. This plan helps me each day in ensuring that my day does not go waste. This keeps me busily working towards achieving my definite chief aim in this life. Just look at the story of creation. God did something each day until He achieved His goal. If you lack a plan, your efforts may come to nothing. Jim Rohn said, *"If you don't design your own life plan, chances are you'll fall into other people's plan; and you know what they have for you. Not much.*

Crystallize your goal and make a plan to achieve them. Set yourself a deadline and with supreme confidence, determination and disregard for obstacles and other people's criticisms, carry out your plan. Napoleon Hill said, *"Create a definite plan for carrying out your desire and begin at once, whether you are ready or not, to put this plan into action."*

Ten Reasons Why You Should Plan

1. *Planning increases an individual's or organization's ability to adapt to future events:*

One of the basic truths about this life is that no one knows what lies ahead. No one knows what tomorrow has in stock. The only thing we can do as humans is to predict the future based on an occurrence or action. Only God knows the future. Apart from that, if anyone would know anything about the future; it might have been revealed to him or her. The future is generally uncertain and things are likely to change with the passage of time. What planning does is to help us adapt to the unexpected when it happens.

There is a story of a rich man whose farm brought forth plenty that he didn't even have enough room to store his produce in Luke 12:16-21. One would realize from this story that it is the man's poor planning that brought him doom. This man forgot to consider planning for the unexpected, since planning involves approaching situations thoughtfully and considering the possibilities and risk at play. He only thought of enjoying what he had produced but failed to consider the fact that he might not even live to enjoy what he had worked for. He thus didn't leave a will or any document showing what should happen to his wealth when he is no more. Just take a look at the question that was asked in the verse 20 of the same chapter, *"then whose shall those things be, which thou hast provided?"* Planning must consist of every possible thing, whether good or bad, so that when it happens we can handle it. Uncertainty is augmented with an increase in the time dimension.

With such a rise in uncertainty there is generally a corresponding increase in the alternative courses of action from which a selection must be made. The planning of activities provides a systematic approach to the consideration of such future uncertainties and events and the planning of activities in terms of what is likely to happen.

2. *Planning helps crystallize objectives:*

The first step in planning is to fix objectives which in turn provides easy course and also gives direction to the activities to be performed. It is in planning that proper objectives are formed. A proper definition and integration of overall and departmental objectives would result in more coordinated and co-operative activities and a greater chance of attaining the overall objectives.

3. *Adequate planning reduces unnecessary pressures of immediacy:*

If activities are not properly planned in anticipation of what is likely to happen, pressures will be exerted to achieve certain results immediately or in a hurry. Thus adequate planning supplies orderliness and avoids unnecessary pressures. When things are planned you know which action or step is next. There are no haphazard moves or actions when there is a good plan. This was one of our greatest challenges when we started our outreaching. Because there was no proper planning, we always confused our activities. We did things any how we thought of until we had learned enough lessons that prompted us to take time to plan before stepping out or doing anything. Now, our activities are grouped and directed. We now know what to do at each time or period anytime we have any program or activity. If time is taking to plan well, there is easy flow of work, and collision among workers is prevented.

4. *Planning reduces mistakes and oversights:*

Although mistakes cannot be entirely obviated, they can certainly be reduced through proper planning. No plan is hundred percent perfect for sure. An expert in planning will tell you that, all plans are altered somewhere along the way, yet this does not make planning irrelevant. Mistakes are bound to come, but if proper planning is done one can reduce the rate at which mistakes occur and can also prevent some of the wounds or hurts caused when mistakes are made.

5. *Planning ensures a more productive use of resources:*

Since planning brings out clarity in objective and also shows what is needed to achieve the needed results, it prevents wasted efforts and resources. A good plan shows both the human resource and financial resource needed to complete an objective. One of the benefits of having a plan before you build a house is that, a quantity surveyor can look at your plan and give you a total estimate of resources needed to finish up the building. Planning will ensure that resources are managed well and not wasted. I got myself in a situation which wore me out seriously due to improper planning. We took many workers than needed to one of our outreach programs and unfortunately for us, we run out of financial resource right in the middle of the campaign owing to the fact that we ignorantly forgot to consider that more workers required more financial input, which we didn't prepare for. When this happened it got us all confused and distracted, and this really affected our efficiency. There were also other times that we misused resources all because we didn't do any proper planning. Good planning results in greater productivity through a better utilization of the resources available to an individual or organization.

6. *Planning makes control easier:*

I was once very fascinated at how one man could supervise a huge construction that was going on without any difficulties when I visited the construction site. But then he made me away of how difficult it will be without a plan. A good plan spells out all objectives and goals as well as also highlighting the controls required. This makes running very easier because with the plan you know which course of action comes first.

7. *Planning helps secure a better position or standing:*

Adequate planning would stimulate improvements in terms of the opportunities available. Just as most banks or financial institutions are ready to help any man or institution with a good business plan, good opportunities come to those who plan their lives. Since good planners are known to mostly excel, they get the best opportunities when they come. Those who plan anything puts themselves in a favorite position of getting the best opportunities available.

8. *Planning enables progress in the manner considered most suitable:*

You make things happen for you exactly how you wanted them to in this life when you can plan well. Since planning outlines objectives and ways you want to get things done, the probability of seeing things go the way you want it is high. And this is because with a plan in place, you will know what exactly to do and what not to do so as to achieve your intended goal. A soccer coach was once asked about how he and his team were able to win one of the most difficult matches they have played. And he joyfully showed how things worked out for them exactly as they planned. If you have a good game plan and you discipline yourself to follow it up, the probability of achieving success is high.

9. *Planning increases the effectiveness:*

The formation and outlining of objectives in planning prevents an individual or institution from doing the wrong or unbeneficial things. This makes you very effective in the achievement of results due to the fact that you are compelled to make decisions on the most appropriate actions to use in order to achieve results. It also prevents repetitions and waste of efforts. Abraham Lincoln is known to have said that he will use six hours to sharpen his axe and then the rest of the two hours to cut down the tree when he is given eight hours to cut down that tree. And I can tell you that decision is the result of a good plan. Since it is known the sharper the axe, the easier and faster it will take him to finish the job. We know that a blunt axe will require much effort and time to finish the job. The actions outline and taken in planning leads to efficiency and effectiveness.

10. *A systematic plan prevents wandering and shortens the road to a goal:*

When you see any individual wandering, then it is either he does not know his destination or does not know the way that leads to his destination. What a good plan does is to show the way to getting something done or achieved. A good plan saves time and resources. The fastest way to get something achieved is to first get hold of the plan that can help you to achieve that. If a plan is like a road map just as H. Stanley Judd suggested, then it makes the journey shorter than it would have been without one.

How to Make a Plan

As much as planning is good, making a good plan is vital and relevant for success. A good plan ensures an effective and successful future. A good plan serves as the blueprint for a successful future, and to have one now will serve you well by leading you to that glorious future you seek. Remember that, the fulfillment of your goal and glorious destiny is not automatic. It requires lots of deliberate actions and efforts. Goal setting, good planning and the ability to follow your goals and plans are some of the prerequisite necessary for a victorious journey to your destiny. And this is what this portion of this book deals with. I believe that everybody has a glorious future, and that the attainment of that future is a possibility. But the only thing left is that good plan which will link each individual to his or her destiny from where he or she is. Below are some points to consider when making any plan for the achievement of any goal:

1. Where you are going?
2. What you require to get there?
3. Where you are currently?
4. How you will get to where you are going?
5. When you intend to get there?

1. *Where are you going?*

This has to do with having a well-defined destination or knowing how the future will look like. Creating a powerful action plan always begins with having a clear purpose, vision or goal in mind. If you don't have any clear cut vision or goal you want to achieve, you will get nowhere. Successful leaders and professionals understand a simple core concept: if you don't know where you're going, you are likely to wind up anywhere. Many people are walking but getting nowhere. And this is because they don't really know where they are going to. To achieve anything worthwhile in this life you have to know what you want. This is one of the differences between the successful and unsuccessful men. Achievers do not only go out for hunting because they want to hunt; they know what they are hunting for. It is important to know what you want to do before you go out doing it. Just imagine meeting someone you know on the street and asking the fellow; "where are you going?" And he replies, "I don't really know!" What will you think or say to that fellow?

You see every step or action in your life becomes useless when it is not targeted towards something. Don't just make any step, make a well calculated step. Make a step that gets you going, towards an intended goal. Don't be like some people out there, who do not really know what they want in this life. Know what you want and go for it. I know before anyone puts up a building, that individual makes a description of the house he or she wants, then based on that description the architect draws the plan for such a structure before construction begins. The same way, we need to know what we want in this life. Don't go to God saying, "well God, anything is okay with me".No! You have to be specific about what you want. David said one thing have I desired, that only will I seek after, that I may dwell in the house of the Lord. This is what I call a prayer of specification. Go to God and speak to Him about that one thing you want to achieve. Don't fuss or fret yourself about anything. Speak to God about that healing ministry, finance organization, business or the industry you desire to have. Make a full description of the exact thing you want on paper, and then go for it with the help of God.

Don't be like those who are going through this life and are ignorant about what they want to be. For them anything is good, provided it will bring them any relief. If they get the chance, they will become everything. Ask these people what they would want to become, and their answer is, they don't know. If they get the chance they will study law. Another time ask them, and they would like to do medicine. Later, they want to be in the army or do some business. This is not how you should live your life. You have to live for something. No one was made for everything. Each individual was made for something in this life. Discover what you were made for and live for that. Do not give up knowing what you stand for in this life. Know your destiny and pursue it.

Have a clear vision or goal and run towards achieving it. This is what makes life worth living; that is when you are living for something. He who lives for nothing is just existing and not living. Your life should be built around purpose. Your purpose in life should be the fulcrum on which you do everything. Don't just run; know what you are running for. Pick a book and pen, and then begin to list the things you desire to achieve in all walks of your life, whether family, professional, and social and health, and then work on them. Is your dream to become a great public speaker or to become a great scientist? Do you have the desire to become an entrepreneur or a billionaire? Just know that whatever you want to become is possible and achievable. The main thing at the beginning is to be sure that, it is what you truly want to be, before you go out chasing it.

2. *What you require to get there*

This explains what one would need to complete his journey to his destination. Every journey has a requirement, and every move has a price to pay. Luke 14: 28 say, ***"for which of you, intending to build a tower, sitteth not downfirst, and counteth the cost, whether he have sufficient to finish?"***

Jesus was in the above verse clearly making all aware of how important it is to first sit down and plan, counting the cost involved before making any move towards building anything. After you get to know where you are going, the next thing to do is to enquire what you require to acquire what you want. There are always some things involved on your way to achievement. What are the requirements? This is common question I believe we should all get used to asking any time we become certain of our definite chief dream. This is because until you know what you require, you might end up doing the wrong things which could cost you. This is one of the major causes of wandering or failure in any given pursuit. If you lack detailed information on what you need to realize your dream, you might never achieve it. This is because you wouldn't know how to achieve it. How can you claim you are preparing for a journey when you don't know its requirements? This means that if you lack details, your preparations will always be inadequate. One of the reasons why I believe Moses sent those twelve men to spy the Promised Land before was to provide adequate information on what they were about to face. Those spies brought exactly the information they were required to bring, though they misinterpreted it. They had adequate information on both the nature of the land and the people dwelling in it. They came out with those possible opportunities which could help them make progress as well as those possible threats and dangers which could also hinder them. This will actually help you with knowing what is involved in the journey you seek to make. I believe that you cannot know how to get to your destination when you don't even know what your journey is required. Ask yourself what you would need to be able to make the journey safely. For example, no one just gets up and decides to travel. You first enquire what you require to get to the very destination you want to go. The same way we all need detailed information on what we require to make our dream come through before we step out. You need to know the resources you need to be to achieve your dream. And some of the things to consider include; educational, spiritual, mental and financial or material needs. This is where we also outline the human resource we believe would need to make our journey. Here also we are able to also outline those treats and opportunities on the way to achieving your pursuit. The treats and opportunities are the things or people on the way that can hinder or help as you press towards your destiny.

3. *Where are you:*

This explains your current location, position or situation in life. This helps you to know the difference between where you are and where you want to go so that you can build the action plan that will lead you to your destination. This involves giving a full description of where you are, how things are and what you have at your disposal. It includes all your foundational elements consisting of your core values, beliefs, principles and ideology. Where do you stand currently in your life? Are you any closer to your dream or goal? If not, what is your strategic positioning on the road to fulfillment? Are you positioned well or not when you consider your destination? Are you positioned well in resources to complete the task of journeying to your dream destination? Here, in the action plan, we give relevance to everything we represent and stand for. This is where we outline our strengths, weaknesses, opportunities and threats so that we will know the strategy to build in order to achieve results. You see most of the things I am communicating to you in this chapter, are things I didn't consider in my early days of ministry, and it led to series of frustrations and disappointments which nearly took my life. My unplanned life and activities only landed me in unnecessary debts and troubles after every outreach program leading to times of pains and sufferings. But when I discovered the blessing in planning everything else changed. God has always got a plan for anything He wants any individual to do for him. Let Him lead or assist you in planning and you will enjoy success. When we started considering planning as an important part of success, our programs, events and outreaches took a new turn. Our programs are now blooming and also debt free. It is getting bigger and powerful as time unfolds. Wonderful things are happening, and we are increasing massively in results. This is because we give time to planning everything before we plunge out. Before I step out to do anything, I consider where I stand. I look at my position financially and the human resource I have. I also look at the gifts at our disposal, our values and beliefs and any other thing that we represent before I look at how we are going to get to our dream goal. After these, I then go ahead to match our strengths and opportunities to build up the strategies that are likely to ensure success. I do not also forget our weaknesses and the possible threats that are also likely to hinder progress or success. By doing this, my team and I are able to build up one of the best action plans which help us to achieve the results we are looking for. Remember that, all that is being treated here is applicable to all fields of endeavor. In order to get to your intended goal, never forget to identify and describe in full where you stand, both in financial resource, machinery, human resource, knowledge, convictions and even in connections, before you ask yourself how to connect your mission to vision. You need to know these things so that you can build up one of the best strategies to achieve your goal. Always knowing where you are, considering your dream goal will help you to know what is involved or what you require to achieve success. Remember that, all things are possible to the man who believes.

4. *How you will get there*:

This explains what to do and how to do it so that success would be achieved. This shows the journey from where you are to where you are going. This is the part of the action plan that layout the roadmap to your intended goal. It consists of the lists of actions and objectives which we build after we take note of our positioning. This is the most important part of an action plan. It is good to know where you are going, but it will be of no use if you do not know how you are going to get there. Knowing how you are going to reach your dream goal is the meat of a strategic plan, but it is also time consuming. This takes a lot of time because there are many routes to your goal, and you will have to be able to pick the right one, which will ensure that you are safer and faster in getting to your goal. In the book of Exodus, the people of Israel were met with two different roads which led to the Promised Land they were marching to, of which one was shorter than the other. The longer one was thirty days longer than the shorter, yet it was the right choice for them. I believe it was the right one not because it was longer, but because it had all that they needed to realize their dream. To have a successful journey to your dream goal, we have a responsibility to choose the right road that best suits our journey. What is important when we get here is not how long or short the road is, but how right it is.

Here, we are to make a list of all the possible actions and then group them into short term goals and strategies. In this way we will be able to check and monitor progress, if we are making some and also know if we are falling out of our plan. Some of these short term actions may include programs jeered at improving ourselves to produce better results. These include personal growth and self-development programs, and other training programs that will sharpen your gifts and abilities for better performances and productivity. Become better and you will do better. Train to become better at what you do, and you will attract better rewards. Training adds value and expertise to your efforts. Excellence is the trade mark of success. Seek excellence by giving yourself the needed training and improvement that will get you going. For example, if you have a dream of becoming a star musician, all you need to do first is give yourself the needed training that will sharpen your gift. You need to make time for rehearsal, practice and other training programs that will build the right attitude in you for a successful journey from where you are to your intended dream goal. After this, go ahead and identify how and where to use your gift so that you will attract the needed help or support. Though the purpose of doing what you know to do with your abilities is not to seek fame, yet your efforts will be reciprocated with many wonderful rewards when people begin to benefit from your gift.

All things are possible to the one who believes. If I say all things, I mean all things. Your dream goal is possible no matter what you have or do not have. Do not be afraid by those things that stand your way to progress. All you need to do is to build up the plan that will take you to your glorious destiny. There is always a way to get through to your intended goal. Let nothing stop you from achievement. You can also do wonders and make anything happen.

5. *When you want to get there*:

This also explains the time duration you want to arrive at your destiny. It is also an important part in the action plan process. It is very important to not only have short term goals but also to set time deadlines to all short term goals. It is not only about how you want to do something but also when you want to get that thing done. Setting time deadline to your goals helps you to check or monitor progress. It also helps you to know the appropriate time or duration to set off to your dream goal.

Chapter 5

DEVELOP AN ATTRACTIVE PERSONALITY

> *Do not follow success; follow excellence and success will follow you …*

To attract means to pull or magnetize something to something. Therefore an attractive personality, here, means a personality which has the ability to pull or magnetize the right things that can ensure successful results. Developing that ability to magnetize is a very important prerequisite to success and achievement in this life. This is due to the fact that we attract almost all the things we get into our lives. The people, favors, support, ideas and all the things which are needed for the fulfillment of our purposes are all attracted. We attract both the bad and the good. Every human has a magnetic field which helps to pull things. But just as some people are naturally attractive and others are not, some individuals have strong magnetic fields of attraction, whiles others have weak magnetic field of attraction. This answers why some people are easily surrounded by people whiles others are not. The greatest blessings each of us can ever get in life are the people we encounter, whether family, friends, and even foes. But much importantly the people you will need to make progress in your life don't just walk into your life, they are attracted to you. This is one of the reasons why self-development is a factor on the way to fulfillment. It increases our magnetic field of influence. If you are a

Pastor, know that the people who become part of your church family are attracted to you.

People won't just come to your church because they don't have anywhere else to go. But they come because there is something about you and your ministry which pulls them to you. Those who don't come to you are not attracted to you. So to have much influence or impact what you should consider doing is to build that attractive personality. You need to work on yourself until you get the results you seek in your ministry, business or institution. On his way to ascending the throne, David needed the right type of men who could help him fight way through. And one day about three hundred men flocked into his life who later became David's mighty men. In the accomplishment of any vision on this planet, people are the most important factor. It is people who will give you the support you require.

The money we get in our business dealings or in our lives do not come from the air but are given by people. That is why most institutions do not joke with both their employees and customers. People are always the most important assets in any vision. This is why you don't just have to lose the right people in your life. Anywhere institutions have lost very key people, whether family, employees or customers, results have drastically reduced. As much as the rise of certain institutions has been dependent on certain key individuals, the fall of others has also been, due to the loss of some keys individuals. It has been said that when the wrong people leave your life, wrong things cease but also when you start losing the right people in your life, the right result or things you once enjoyed go down.

Please note that it is not all the help, people or favors that eludes you that God does not want you to have. You repelled most of them. What you don't attract, you can't keep or experience in your life. Your level of attraction determines your level of influence and results. The quality of things you attract into your life as an individual is dependent on the strength of your magnetism. Sorry to say this; but many people will continue to be helpless in life if they don't make changes in their personality which can fetch them the needed help. You have had people always walked in and out of your life several times and you have been wondering why. You drove most of them away yourself.

If you can have a successful run to your intended destination, you will need to build this personality if you don't have one. Are you not surprise at why certain people are pursuing their destinies alright yet look helpless and lonely though they are doing their best to get on in life? I know men and women who had people come to work for them, but they are now lonely due to this very reason. The type of personality you have in life is a prerequisite to success. I am not so surprised that David, even whiles on exile as a result of the pursuance of King Saul, still had people following him. The Bible said he was attractive, and it is obvious that this was a contributing factor. Develop yourself into a sweet and attractive individual, and you will attract what you need to advance. Just as most men like to follow very beautiful and attractive ladies, good people and things will follow the one who is both a spiritual, psychological and physical beauty. Develop that beauty in both your spirit and soul, and let it continue reflecting in you no matter what. And you will make good contacts and connection very soon.

What You Are Is Important

It is obvious that this book is basically on self-development. You can see that right from the beginning of the first chapter I have not ceased to elaborate on it and this is because it is the greatest secret to making and enjoying life. God does not only want you to develop your gifts, abilities and potentials to succeed. He also wants you to develop your spirit, attitude and personality in order to have an unceasing success. Success is not only built on gifts, your personality too matters. Many people have used wrong methods in gaining wealth and affluence in life. And this has caused the world serious harm, in that, many wrong person are handling good things. When slaves are riding on horses and princes are walking, there is surely something wrong. The Bible say, ***when the wicked bears rule, the people mourn, but when the righteous is in authority the people rejoice*** (Proverbs 29:2). In other words when a wrong person rules a nation, the citizens suffer. A wrong person in this case is someone who is either underdeveloped or undeveloped in character or personality, though he or she might be gifted. An undeveloped man both in character and mindset cannot develop a nation. That has been the problem of the undeveloped nations of the world. The development you get in your physical life is only a reflection of the mental or personality development you have. Self-development is an important key in any success story but unfortunately it has been neglected by many for cheap ways and methods which do not produce any lasting results. Many have fallen for that great lie in this world today which says, "*What you have determines how successful you are.*" And so most have spent their lives accumulating and amassing wealth through all sorts of means. Understand that life is not about gathering, it is about what and who you are. The true measure of success is by what you are than what you have. This is why it is important to consider personal development above all else. First of all, learn to become what you want to experience, and they will follow you. In the bible Jesus indicated that signs and wonder shall follow those who believe. He never stressed that those who believe would follow sings and wonders, which is not what is happening today. Today, many are pursuing signs and wonders almost everywhere you go and I believe this is so because we have failed in understanding that remarkable statement made by Jesus in Mark 16:15. This is an issue of development. That believer Jesus was talking about is that individual who has had his perceptions, values, virtues, beliefs and ideals about himself, others, life and the world as a whole changed as a result of his believe in Jesus.

Again, to believe in Jesus, means, to accept His ideals about life in general, embrace his mindset, character and values. In other words become like Jesus, and those signs and wonders He talked about will follow you. If you don't see those signs following you, then it means that, you are still holding on to your old self, beliefs, ideals, and virtues. But if you want the signs which followed Jesus in His earthly walk to follow you, then you need to work on yourself so as to become that person whom those signs are likely to follow. So the key to attracting the best things in life is in personality development. Don't follow success but follow becoming a better person in your field of endeavor and then the success will follow you. The best way to have wealth is to develop your personality. The material possessions only become a product of what you become. This is not to say that it is not important to have wealth. What you should note is that what an individual becomes is directly and greatly linked to what he or she has. I mean what you are determines what you will have. This is something that should be revered. If gathering or amassing wealth is the actual measure of success, then those who through evil means gather wealth are successful. But it is never so. A truly successful man is what he is. Don't let this truth go unutilized. What you are, is important than what you have. Let this sink deep into your subconscious, never to be forgotten. Just refuse to be part of the many that are living with the deception that success is all about gathering. It is an undisputable fact that this world places great importance to the accumulation of wealth, and most times ignores self-development, yet it does not change the truth. All those who walk in this delusion later on end up as victims at the end of the road. A lasting success is far better than a temporal one, and permanent enjoyment is better. The one who spends his entire life gathering is nowhere to be compared to the man who spends his life developing himself into the success he wants.

This world is full of people who are trying to gather their way to affluence whereas; some few others are attracting billions by each day. And this is because they have developed themselves to get that. You don't get what you want in life but what you are. When you discover that what come into your life are negative things, you have to understand that you are negative as a person and needs to change. A negative person attracts negative results, whereas a positive person attracts positive results. That is the measure of your true wealth. Anybody can accumulate or have material wealth, by whatever means possible. Some kill to have wealth, while others cheat to have it. Several others steal or rob to amass wealth and others through corrupt practices or through inheritance get it. So the process of gathering is never a sure base in declaring someone as wealthy. A person who kill to have money, is a killer, and not wealthy, so is a person who steal to gather wealth a thief and not rich. Your person matters than your possessions.

You can lose your possessions, but if you have a wealthy or rich personality, you regain everything. Your non material resources play a greater role on the road to fulfillment than your material resources. Build your personality and then success will follow you. What you are made up of, is relevant if you will make a mark in this life. Your content is the greatest blessings you can ever have. Your constitution can never be ignored if you will make it to any great feat. True wealth is about your non material resources which include knowledge, belief, enthusiasm, willingness, courage, faith, life, desire, creativity, skill, time and a good fighting spirit. Your wealth is you. It has been agreed by almost all the greatest philosophers since the beginning of time that; what you are is more important than what you have. And I also agree to this fact. Are you asking me why I agree? Well, I agree because that is exactly what the word of God teaches. Mankind's problem had always been his being than his deeds. That is why God changed our being by giving us a new image in Christ Jesus (2 Corinthians 5:7). As Christians our wealth is on the inside. We have a rich spiritual personality, and the active development of what we are on the inside leads to a great life on the outside. What you are is important if you will make any mark anywhere.

All the material resources or blessings that flow into your life are the by-products of what you are. You are really your wealth. Henry

Ford was once asked, what he would do if he loses all his wealth, and this was the answer he gave, "Give me three years and I will regain everything I have lost." Was this a proud statement? No! It was instead a confident statement, a statement of faith in who he was or what he had become. He knew that his wealth was not the material things he had acquired but himself. In his book 'Church Growth,' Dr. Yonggi Cho also made this similar statement "take me to any place in this world and I will get the same results in church growth as I have here." These men could make this statement as a result of this one fact; they had become their wealth. It was not just the outward or material success they had achieved but what they had become. What you are, really matters in the school of progress. If you want to understand who you are, just check what you are attracting. Success is not tied to just an environment but to personality. That is why God is most times not interested in changing the circumstance, but interested in changing you. Because when you change, the problem will cease. Most people are their trouble in life. They focus and waste their energies worrying about problems instead of finding the solutions. Improve yourself and your life will improve. Build and make conscious investments in your personality, and you will reap good returns. Spend time and resources developing yourself and you will make great progress in this life. Like David, you need to build up a personality that attracts. Please understand that this is not automatic. It requires conscious efforts. The Bible makes it clear that David had an attractive personality, and this became part of the qualities which won Saul's approvable. You are also your wealth. Just look at yourself and think about the results you are reflecting in your life. Seek and begin to build that mindset and character which can aid you to attract the results you want and you will reflect in your life. Never forget this truth; you don't get what you want in life but what you are. You easily get what you are. The law of attraction says that everyone attracts to himself what he thinks. And the Bible too says as a man thinketh so he is. So in other words you attract to yourself what you are. Your person is important than your possessions. You may fake your deeds but cannot hide what you are. It will surely surface for all to see. It is not just aptitude but attitude. It is not about what you are doing but who you are.

Improve Your Personality

There is an interesting story about a certain town which had only three wealthy men. These three men owned all the businesses, factories, institutions and major projects in town and had all the men of that town working for them. One day all the men working for these three wealthy men requested for increment in their salaries and allowances but were denied. So out of fury, they all marched to the king of their town, petitioning that these three wealthy men who were deemed by them as cruel should be exiled from the town and their wealth taken over by the township. When their king heard this, he became troubled and confused, and this was because he knew that the entire township had benefited from these men. They were responsible for most of the developmental projects of the town, had built institutions which had provided jobs for his people and had been very supportive to the king. So how could he be cruel to them in this way? Since he didn't know what to do, he invited an old wise man in the town for his counsel. When the old wise man heard this he smiled and told the king that the best way to solve the issue was to sit the three men down and ask them to present their wealth, after which the king should divide them equally and share among all the men in the town. These three wealthy men readily agreed when they were invited. So the king divided and shared all the wealth of these three rich men among all the men in the town. But after three years the king noticed something which bothered him the more. Those three men had become three times richer and the men of the town poorer than they were three years before. Since the king didn't understand why it was so, he invited the old wise man to know why it was so. Then the old wise man made the king aware that, the problem was not with the three wealthy men but with all the men of the town. They had gotten the wealth of those three men but not what made those men wealthy. That was why it ended like that and by this way everyone has seen that every man is his own problem. What makes the rich man wealthy is his mindset and character, just as it is the poor man's mindset and character that makes him poor.

With the story above I want you my reader to know and understand that the secret of successful men in achieving success is in the development of their personality. This is one of the reasons why the rich keeps getting richer and the poor, poorer. A poor man is not a man without material wealth but one without the right type of mindset and character. And this is because the material wealth we get in our lives is reflection of who we are. Stop chasing after success and pursue the development of your personality, and success will follow you soon. Know that all those things most people are running after in the world today are meant to be added if you build the right type of personality, according to Matthew 6: 33. In other words, the one who excels in the building of kingdom attributes will attract kingdom success. Build a successful personality and you will experience a successful life. Develop yourself and you shall not only be blessed but be a channel of blessing to others.

As believers, God has given us an image that has the capacity of attracting any blessing we desire in this life, if only we would develop ourselves into that image. According to the revelation of the new birth, we already have deposited in our spirits all the personality traits which ensure success. What we are expected to do is to develop these traits which already lay in our spirit before we have influence. Success will come to the man who makes time to develop these attitudes into His personality. The reward after self-development is seriously immense, so spend time and effort in becoming a better person each day.

Develop out of your innerman the virtue of righteousness, peace, joy, love, faith, patience, honesty, courage, longsuffering, meekness, gentleness, kindness, desire, heart for knowledge and wisdom, and endurance, and there is nothing you cannot achieve.

Self-development always precedes achievement. God subjects every individual to a process of development before attainment. Develop a good relationship with people and learn how to flow with everyone. Remember that success is not achieved alone. You need the right people, your enemies notwithstanding to be able to get to your destination. People are important than things in this life. You need people to make it in life. Whoever puts relevance to things than people is an active failure.

Your first record of success should be in the area of your relationship with people before any other. The one who succeeds in this will succeed anywhere in his life. If you know how to relate well with people then you are a good candidate for success. Life is mainly about people and not things. That is why you need to be attractive so as to get the right people into your life. You need the virtue of love, honesty, faithfulness, faith, tolerance, longsuffering, meekness, goodness, temperance, patience and respect for others. The bible says in 2 Peter 1: 8, that, if any man gives time and effort to developing these virtues, he will neither be barren nor unfruitful. He shall be productive. These virtues are what will help you in your relationship with other people, whether family, friends, workers, employer or employee, customers, or associates.

How to Develop Your Personality

To improve your personality, there are three areas about your person you need to consider. And they are your mindset, character and appearance.

Mindset

The first thing to look at is to seek to improve your mindset or mentality. Mindset is said to be a habitual mental attitude. It can also be said to be the way your mind is set or programmed to behave both consciously and unconsciously in interpreting or responding to situations or the events of life. The Central Processing Unit (CPU) of your computer is the brain of your computer which helps it to perform every task you want from the machine. Yet without a software installation, you can't operate the machine. And how the machine is programmed to operate is how it is set to perform. Similarly, the human brain is the hardware but the mind is the software the brain needs to operate. It is the type of mind you have that will determine the kind of life you will enjoy. Your mental condition determines your living condition. This makes mindset development the most important thing to consider working on if you desire a wonderful life in this world.

According to psychologists, the human mind is made up of three main parts, which are the conscious, subconscious and unconscious. It is by these three main parts that the mind is able to work to produce results in our lives.

The conscious mind has to do with the awareness of our current environment or things. For example, you are aware of your current environment, the chair you are seated on now or your current activity. It communicates through speech, images, movements and thoughts.

The subconscious mind has to do with where certain thought or information which you are not aware of currently but can easily be reached out for when needed is stored. You are not thinking about your phone number now, but you can recall it when needed. This is where all recent memories are stored for quick recall when needed, such as what your house address is, or the name of someone you just met.

The unconscious mind is the storage place for all memories and programs that have been installed since you were born. It is the storehouse of all your deep seated emotions, habits, behaviors and memories. This is where you will locate all the experiences you have had since birth. And it is from this that your beliefs, habits and behaviors are formed and reinforced over time. Memories in your unconscious mind cannot be easily accessed by choice like the subconscious. It is only triggered by certain events or experiences.

This is not a book on the mind but it is very important for you to get this. Knowing how the mind works will easily help you to build the right mindset for the life you want. It is your mental programing which determines whether you become a pessimist or an optimist. Optimists are those who have positive view of life and things, whereas pessimists have negative views about everything. Optimists have a "can do" attitude whereas pessimists have the "can't do" attitude. Optimists are winners and those who are always making things happen in this world whereas pessimists end up as losers and victims in the same world. These are the two main categories of people in life. And this is the result of our mental programing. Both pessimists and optimists are that way because of what and how their minds were program.

The following will help you in building a good mindset for a powerful life:

- Choose the right thoughts: Martin Luther King Jr. said that, "*you cannot stop birds from flying over your head but you can keep them from building their nest in your hair.*" There are hundreds of thoughts flying through our minds each minute. There are good and bad, clean and unclean, and several others like thoughts of fear, disappointment, deception and many others but what you dwell or focus on is what sinks into your memory and finally become a part of your unconscious mind. You cannot stop these thoughts from flying into your mind, but you can choose which to dwell on. Apply your conscious mind to clean, positive and victorious thoughts. Refuse to dwell on negative thoughts. Practice focusing the mind on positivity.

- Seek Education: to be educated is to empower your mind with the right information. This is another way you can build a quality mindset for quality life. Any mindset or mentality whether of an optimist or pessimist is the result of the information such individual received from his or her environment and had dwelt on for most of his life. These may include information received from both painful and happy experiences or events that happened in one's life, certain occurrences from childhood, stories or tales from parents or friends, advice, and many more. If the information you got and dwelt on while growing up is negative, that is how your mindset becomes. There is a term in IT which says, *"Garbage in, garbage out."* The output is never different from the input. If the information you received is good then that is the life you will produce. But if it is bad or negative it still can be changed by re informing the mind with the right information. Be informed with the right information and you will perform. Information will help you to correct wrong beliefs, values and ideals. One of the reasons why I will forever be grateful to Jesus Christ for making me a Christian is that Christianity has brought me great change. It changed my self-ideals, self-image and self-esteem. It also changed my perception about life, people and gave me a different view of the world. And this happened after I gave myself to God's Word through study and learning. Be transformed by renewing your mind with the revelation of God's Word.

Until those negative beliefs, ideals and values of yours change, the negative things you experience in life will keep happening. Think clean, positive thoughts and the results will be visible. Develop positive thought patterns about yourself, others and about life.

Appearance

How you appear also speaks lots of volumes of about you. It is true that you cannot judge a book by its cover, but the cover design and title of the book can make people salivate to read the book. Before you get the opportunity to impress the people you meet in life with your attitude or character, your first impression will be from your appearance. How you look is very important and has everything to do with how success comes to you. One of the ways people will get attracted to you is by how you look. Your personal branding is dependent on your appearance. And the branding you give yourself is what others will use to describe you. Paul once said, he became like the Jews when in the midst of Jews and also became like non-Jew, when he was in the midst of non-Jews, so that he could win many people to Christ. This same principle works today. If you desire good things or people in your life, then look good. Remember that you always attract into your life what you are. Look neat and dress good. I do not mean you should be extravagant. Be simple, yet attractive in your field of endeavor. Appear like a conqueror.

Love

There is a scriptural verse in the Bible that says that, ***"whoever claims to love God yet hates a borther or sister is a liar"*** 1 John 4:20. It goes on to say that you claim to love God though you don't see him, but hates the brother you see. This and other verses in the bible clearly shows that the one who loves God, truly love his brother. Loving God goes beyond singing, praying, studying the word and even preaching. Love is one of the virtues that attract people to us. Mankind is made to respond to the call of love. I am a Christian, and this is, because I responded to God's love call in John 3: 16. It says, ***"For God so loved the world, that he gave his only begotten Son, that whosoever believeth in him should not perish, but have everlasting life."*** John 3:16.

Love has such beauty and power to pull men of all kinds to itself.

No one is designed to be an island on his own. Success or greatness is not achieved alone. We are all made to depend on each other. The big needs the small, the strong the weak, the disabled the abled, the rich the poor and vice versa. Destiny's wheels are not driven alone. Two are always better than one, but you need to be attractive enough to get the other one in other to be two. Successful marriage or relationship is not possible without that force of attraction. Attraction is an important element to union. Love is the only bond that binds any two together. It always unites people and empowers them to walk and work together. Love's way has always won. Love and care for people, and they will help you to do anything. That is why we were admonished by God's Word to love all and even our enemies. This is the only way we will have people to walk and work with us.

You need people in your life and on your way to fulfillment, just as David needed his mighty men on his way to the throne. And love is one of the greatest forces that will draw and bind people to you. Men will come to you uninvited and assist you achieve success when they see that you are a man of love. This is what happened to David. The people who became his men were not invited by him, they came to him themselves. They were men and people who left their homes and towns to join him when he himself had nowhere to live and was living in caves.

David therefore departed thence, and escaped to the cave Adullam: and when his brethren and all his father's house heard it, they went down thither to him.

And everyone that was in distress, and everyone that was in debt, and everyone that was discontented, gathered themselves unto him; and he became a captain over them; and there were with him about for hundred men (1 Samuel 22:1-2).

Did you notice the people who came and how they came to David? They were men in distress, debt and were not happy with their various situations. And they came willingly, uninvited and made David their boss. This is what I want you to see. When people see that their destinies are secured with you, they wouldn't mind leaving all to follow you. I believe this was what the people saw. They saw in David someone who would care for their wellbeing, someone who would help and lead them into being who they were really meant to be. These men were just ordinary men in society who didn't mean much to anybody. They were poor, miserable and irrelevant but their lives later became history. Most of them became the mighty men of David. They became champions and heroes in war and life. I believe this was what they saw. Everybody needs somebody in their lives. David needed these men as much as they needed him. But people will only come to you when they see around you the environment that can sustain and build them up. And that is a love environment. If they see that you care and love them unconditionally, they won't mind you being their boss. But if they see that you despise and underrate them, they will leave you. Love is one of the virtues in a man which attracts.

Love people and people will come to you. I personally have encountered lots of people who personally came to work with me even when I had not invited them. People will always troop to where they would feel loved and comforted. When they see that you respect them no matter whom and where they are, they will be willing to die for you. Nobody loves to be in hostile environment. Love people, and get people. Hate people and you will lose people. What you love comes into your life. Love and respect people for what and who they are. You need the people in your life to get to that throne of destiny. Just make them feel relevant and wanted and they will give you all they are and have. If you don't treat them well they will leave you. Everything in this life revolves around people, so love people. Don't live for material things, and disrespect people.

The Golden Rule

This rule says that, "Do to others what you would want others to do unto you." This is one of the profound truths Jesus taught in His earthly ministry. Whatever you do to others, you would have same done to you. It is a rule that binds life. Do good to people, and people will do good to you. Love people and people will love you. Your actions and deeds in the life towards others are like seeds that are being sown. And you will definitely reap whatever you sow in this life. Those who spend time and effort, making other people happy, will also be made happy. The Bible says, "...***He that watereth shall be watered also***" Proverbs 11:25b. What you do to others never goes in vain. Plant a seed of joy in the lives of people and make them happy. Be selfless in your dealing with people and not selfish, whether at home, work, or in society. Do not use people for your personal gains and dump them later. Selfish people don't achieve greatness, so avoid it. Help those around you to achieve their dream too. The kind of example many have set is very bad in society and are not worthy of emulation. They use people to get things, and not things for people. They don't care what goes on in the lives of others. All they care about is their own welfare and success. I once heard an employer abusing his employee for complaining about their poor conditions of service. Seeing a man abuse his fellow when he was cheating him and his colleagues of what was due them was very pitying but I wasn't so surprised. This is because these things are common occurences.

Keep doing this to your fellow man and life will give you back what you are giving to people. Be fair to each other. Treat your fellow man well, and others will treat you well. Give to others what is due them, and don't take from others what is not yours. If you work for somebody, do what is expected of you, and do it well, and you shall be rewarded. Don't do somebody's work anyhow, and expect good reward. Do it as if it was your own. Be sincere and honest in your dealings with men and in your businesses. Let your yes be yes and your no, no. Eschew evil and corrupt practices and help people when necessary. Before you do anything to anybody, first pause and ask yourself whether you will be happy if others do the same thing to you. Employees, who steal company properties, ask yourself whether you will be happy if that was your company. You report at work at any time you like and you don't care. Also ask yourself whether you would be happy if others do that to you. I once met a pastor cursing his associate for breaking away from his church to start his own with about half of his congregation and I wasn't so shocked because this pastor once did the same thing to his senior pastor. Never forget this; whatever you do to others will be done to you and you will even reap more than what you sow in life. Give your best shots and skill to help move the work you do for others, and please don't break their hearts. Even if the one who enjoyed from your act of good deed pays you with evil, this life will ensure that you get a just return for your deed in a different way in this life. What you do to others is always done unto you. Don't cheat, steal, rob, kill, lie or bear false witness. Be a brother or sister to your fellow. Be happy for them when they are progressing and you too will progress. Don't abuse others with your words just because you are good at talking, rather encourage and inspire them with your words. Let your words be seasoned with salt; in other words it should bless and preserve and not hurt or break. Learn to be the first person in people's lives to help them up, when they fall. Have pity on people and show mercy. Forgive others for the wrongs they do to you and do not be vengeful.

Faith

This is one of the few virtues which can bring people to you. People like to be around someone who is getting results. When a man's ideas are working, he is the one people will troop to watch and listen. Mankind applauds achievers and champions. When a man has something to show as a witness to his exploits he will easily get a hearing. And it takes faith to produce results. It is faith that saves, delivers and yield positive or better results. Faith will save your face. Do you know that even the Bible admonishes men to follow the faith of those whose lives have produced results (Hebrews 13:7)? It is only faith that wins a following. No man will bother himself with coming to follow ordinary men or a man who is full of fear. Those four hundred men, who left their homes to follow David, knew they were not just following an ordinary man, but someone whose faith had produced results. Nobody wants a man of fear as a leader, but a man of faith. People will easily follow a daring man or a man who can urge them on to achievement using himself as an example. It said that this is one of the acts of Alexander the Great, which contributed in his having such a great military following leading to capturing almost half of the then known world. Men do not follow fearful men but men full of faith. It is said that whatever action a great man performs, common men follow; and whatever standards he sets by exemplary acts, all the world pursues. History has always proven that it is only champions who are cheered. This was why the women sang those songs to David after he slew Goliath instead of Saul, their King. Nobody wants a failure as model. You can check from society, everybody's role model is a winner or hero. And everyone wants to work with those who can be of help to them. Don't be jealous when no one is following you, you probably have not achieved anything. The Bible says *"**The poor are shunned even by their neighbors, but the rich have many friends**"* Proverbs 14:20 NIV. The rich man is the one who has produced results, especially financial results, and the Bible says he has many friends. This is so because he is seen as an inspiration to many, and most people won't even think if they are handed the opportunity of serving or working with them. One of the reasons why I am a follower of Jesus Christ is because He is a winner and he has made me such when I gave myself to following Him. What I want you to understand is that when men see that you are producing results, they will follow you or would want to be with you. And it is only faith that produces positive results.

Men of faith are men of uncommon acts and are praise worthy. It is not only people or mankind who are attracted to faith; God is also attracted to the man of faith. As a faith God he works with a faith man. God is not pleased with fear or unbelief; He is only pleased with faith. Great faith produces great results. Look through the pages of history and you will see that nothing great happened without faith. The whole chapter of Hebrews 11 is a confirmation on this. Even

God needed faith to get things done. The chapter goes on to say that the world is understood to have been framed by the Word of God through faith. In other words it takes faith to create your world. Today all Christians read the book of Hebrews 11 because it is a great source of motivation to living a life full of faith. Most Christian leaders use that part as a great inspiration to faith when urging their followers on in faith.

Things to Consider

1. Love people and use things, don't love things and use people. Let people be so important to you than things. Your human resource is the most important part of whatever organization or institution you are building, so treat them well. Hear me; the profit you want to make is good but not as important as both the people (employees) you need to help you and those (customers) to bring those profits. Let your priority be, Purpose, Plan, People and then Profit and not the other way round. It is always people before profit. If you treat people well, they will be willing to help you achieve your dreams.

2. Be interested in people and show concern for what goes on in their lives. Get close and know what they are doing with their lives. Do your best to know what their visions, aims and objectives in life are, and help them achieve them. Don't be jealous when the Lord is blessing them; instead be happy for what the Lord is doing in their lives. Don't leave them in times of trouble or sorrow. Be the one to comfort them. The Bible says to mourn with them who mourn, and rejoice with them who rejoice. When you see others grieving, be the one to encourage them.

3. Be flexible and open minded. You need to be flexible enough to adapt to new conditions in life, and accept new ideas. No one knows it all, so be willing to learn from others. If you are too rigid in life you will break soon. Learn from especially those who are ahead of you and be opened to wise counsel

4. Respect other people's feeling and learn not to hurt them. Do not be insensitive to their emotional demands. Also be courteous

5. Learn to inspire and motivate others. We all need inspiration and motivation at one point in our lives. A great man once said that the one who lives without any inspiration will soon expire. I know that without inspiration and motivation some of us would have faded off. Inspiration brings the life back when things go down and everything looks dead. Inspiration is filling someone with a quickening or exalting influence. It is to influence or impel someone to achievement. If you as a leader need this, then know that those around you too will need it. And please do not deny them, when they need your inspiration. Lift them up when they are down, encourage and inspire faith in them when they are discouraged.

6. Smile always because it cheers others and draws many to you. It is said smiling is very contagious. This always helps people out of some emotional pressure and brings relief and hope in the place of despair. Research shows that, smiling releases pleasure hormones called endorphins and antidepressant hormones called serotonin. Smile does not only affect other people positively, it affects you too. It sends positive message to your being, that life is good. Whiles frowns repel people from you, smiling attracts people.

7. Master all negative emotions and use all good emotions well. Learn to control negative emotions and prevent yourself from hurting others with them. Do not act angrily towards people when you feel anger. Make good use of positive emotions and educate yourself in mastering the negative ones. Just as I always tell my readers, don't do what you feel like, do what is required and important. Control your anger, frustrations, sorrows, depression, disappointments and all the other negative emotions you feel. Learn how not to make others victims of your negative emotions.

8. Help people to solve their problems and lend a helping hand where necessary. People admire problem solvers not problem carriers. And people are willing to reward the man who has answers and solutions.

9. Check the way you speak to people and also watch carefully your choice of words.

10. Develop a positive mental attitude towards yourself and the people who comes into your life

11. Be happy and joyful yourself. Look, you cannot make others happy in life when you are not. People must drink from your fullness. You cannot be to people what you are not. And how can you give what you don't have. The Bible admonishes us to rejoice always which is very important and useful to us.

12. Build people and don't destroy them. Bring the best in them and lead them to success. Teach them to fish and don't just fish for them always. Help them attain all the training they require to do wonders in life.

13. Respect people, give honor to whom honor is due, tribute to whom it is due and give to people what is due them. Don't cheat people of what is due them.

Chapter 6

DEVELOP A GOD CONSCIOUSNESS

"...and the Lord is with him" 1 Samuel 16:18

This is the greatest, as well as one of the most important of all the keys to success outlined in this book – developing a consciousness of the presence of God. It was *the* greatest secrets of all the successful men the Bible mentions as well as some of the greatest individuals recorded in the history of humanity. Today, it is still the same, that wherever individuals have had the backing and support of God, uncommon successes have been achieved. If you are an atheist reading this book I want you to understand that someone created the universe and established those laws which governs it. He is God Almighty. May be you don't accept this because the Bible says so but this is reality. Today, many top scientists have come out to say that truly there is a God up there who made the universe due to some of their findings. But to us this is nothing new because of the fact that the Bible has already said it.

Romans 1:20 says, *"For the invisible things of him from the creation of the world are clearly seen, being understood by the things that are made, even his eternal power and Godhead ..."* So, when scientists come out later to inform us that according to study, they now believe that there is a monotheistic God who made the universe and keeps it together, it is not surprising to us. This is because the above verse clearly shows that by the things God made, they will understand. So when physicists by studying the universe come out to prove the existence of God, it is not shocking to us. Over the years many top scientists have come out to support the existence of God. Below are quotes from some of them;

"The more I study science, the more I believe in God." Albert Einstein

"God is the author of the universe and the free establisher of the laws of motion" Robert Boyle (Pharmacist and Chemist who is considered to be the father of modern chemistry)

"It may seem bizarre, but in my opinion science offers a surer path to God than religion." Paul Davies

"Astronomers now find they have painted themselves into a corner because they have proven, by their own methods, that the world began abruptly in an act of creation to which you can trace the seeds of every star, every planet, every living thing in this cosmos and on earth. And they have found that all this happened as a product of forces they cannot hope to discover … That there are what I or anyone would call supernatural forces at work is now, I think a scientifically proven fact." Robert Jastrow (astronomer, physicist and founder of NASA's Goddard Institute of Space)

I can go on and on writing quotes or comments made by renowned scientists both past and present showing their beliefs that there is a God who owns the universe but the above quotes are enough to help you understand that science does not disprove the existence of God. Lord William Kelvin, who was noted for his theoretical work on thermodynamics once said, *"If you study science deep and long enough, it will force you to believe in God."* Science proves the existence of God, though most scientists describe Him as a Force and others call Him Energy. We know by scripture that it is not just an energy or force at work but a Supreme Being. He is the God of the universe and everything in it.

Science has really helped humanity but I believe that if there is any book or manuscript to inform us about the God of the universe, then it is the Bible. Because before science came out to mention the existence of a monotheistic God who holds the universe together and sets the entire universe in order and harmony, the Bible had already mentioned and given some detail about Him. Genesis 1:1 says *"in the beginning God created the heaven and the earth,"* whereas Psalm 148:2– 6 clearly shows that the sun, moon and stars were made and established by God. Colossians 1:16 says, "*for by him were all things created, that are in heaven, and that are in earth, visible and invisible, whether they be thrones, or dominions, or principalities, or powers: all things were created by him and for him*".

Before science spoke about the unseen force which holds the universe together, the verse 17 of Colossians chapter 1 and other verses in the Bible had already indicated that it was God's power that holds the universe together. It was God who established the laws that governs nature. We don't just know that He exists, we know Him by name. He is the one who "...*appeared unto Abraham, unto Isaac and unto Jacob by the name* **'God Almighty'** and to Moses and the children of Israel as **'Jehovah'** Exodus 6:3. We know that He does not only want to be the God of the universe but also of the people He created to inhabit His earth in this universe. In the book of Jeremiah, He says, *"and they shall be my people, and I will be their God"* Jeremiah 32:38. He again promises in Leviticus 26:12 to walk among humanity and be their God. It says, *"and I will walk among you, and will be your God, and ye shall be my people."*

Isn't this awesome, that the God who made the universe seeks to be with and help humanity live life to the fullest? Whoever scripture showed to have had the privilege of knowing and associating with this great God, came out strong, successful and victorious in all things in this life. The greatest blessing that anyone can ever have in life is to know and be connected to God.

Interestingly He comes to help men who align themselves with Him in the fulfillment of what He made them for. Life itself is not complete if you don't have God. It is not enough to have only physical or natural things of life. There are things in the spiritual realm far above this natural realm you need to know and have to make life complete, of which the greatest is to know and associate with the Creator of the universe and everything in it. I can boldly say that anyone who lacks God is at risk. You can develop all the virtues outlined in this book but if you lack that spiritual presence of God, you are in danger.

Most successful men have mentioned that they believe that there was an unseen force behind their success and the breakthrough this world has enjoyed in every field of endeavor. People have always come out to testify about how, when all hope was gone, something they knew very well couldn't have happened naturally happened to save certain situations. And they believe it was a greater force aiding and assisting. The Supreme Being has always been at work wherever people have given themselves wholly to Him or have aligned themselves with Him. His wonderful hand has always been in most inventions and discoveries which have blessed this world.

Top scientists, who once didn't believe in the existence of God, today have used scientific approach or formulas to prove the existence of God. My greatest focus in this chapter is to show you how God has been the biggest secret and reason behind all the good successes the world has enjoyed.

Partnering With God

"We then as workers together with him..." 2 Corinthians 6:1

Partnership has been one of the easiest ways to get things achieved in this world. Two are always better than one. Any wise united or collaborative effort does wonders. It is said in the Bible that, one shall chase thousand but two shall chase ten thousand. That means when two agree to do anything the result is remarkable. When two people pray in agreement, God has said in His word that He will answer. It is not good for a man to be alone. Every individual need company on the way to fulfillment. Nobody achieves success alone. And the type of company you keep determines the kind of progress you make towards destiny. The emphasis in this session of the book is on keeping a spiritual company, not just physical one. As much as people are a great factor in life, you cannot do away with the God factor. He is the greatest you need to achieve your dream. The Bible says with Him all things are possible. The impossible becomes achievable when you enter into partnership with God.

Maybe you are asking whether it is possible to be in partnership with God as suggested above. And I want you to understand that it is possible. When people accepts, cooperate, master and do His will and bidding, we say that they partnered with God.

This was David's secret. The Bible says, ***"David waxed greater and greater: for the Lord of host was with him"*** (1 Chronicles 11:9). This was how unskillful men and women made impact in the scriptures. If there is anyone to fear in life, fear the one in partnership with God. If God is against you, woe, but if He is with you and for you, then be ready to do exploits. Your geographical location won't matter if God is with you. You will make impact wherever you find yourself. Like Daniel and the other three Hebrew young men, you can do the uncommon if God is with you. Seek God and get connected to Him. Relate with Him and let Him assist you. This is one of the surest ways to reach that place of glory. I prefer to have God and not have people rather than have people and not have God, though having God will bring the right people you need to fulfill your destiny.

The history of how Israel in the Bible defeated great nations on their way to the Promised Land is a great example of how you can walk throughout life undefeated if you have God on your side. It was through the help of the God of the universe that they were freed from slavery in the first place. And then it was with His help that they were able to defeat the Amalekites. God was the only reason why they could bring down the walled city of Jericho in the book of Joshua 6. If not for God, how would anyone explain how on earth just three hundred military men could defeat millions of Medians, Amalek and military men from the east in Gideon's day (Judges 7). The people of Israel became a force to reckon with, all because they had alliance with the great God who made the universe. He was the secret to their defense then and now despite the enormous enemies surrounding them. Whoever feared them back then feared them because of their God. Listen to what the Philistines said when they heard that the ark of covenant which represented the presence God was in the camp of the army of Israel in 1 Samuel 4:7, 8, "...*woe unto us! Who shall deliver us out of the hand of these mighty Gods? These are the Gods that smote the Egyptians with all the plagues in the wilderness*". "*Blessed is the nation whose God is the Lord*", says the Bible in Psalm 33:12. Just like the wife of Haman and his wise men told him concerning Mordechai, if you meet any man who is associated with God do not take him for granted. The man who has God's supernatural help and assistance will always be unstoppable. Good things are reserved for all by the grace of God, yet it takes men who partners with God to access them. If you think that may be you have enjoyed success without Him, you are deceiving yourself. Except those who through evil means got what they want, whatever we receive in life, is given to us by God. This same God is ready to help anyone who comes to Him for help. He is ready to assist you fulfill your mission on earth. All you have to do is to simply call on Him. Whether you know Him or not, He knows you by name.

One of the reason why He is the best you can partner with is that He knows you more than you know yourself, and this is because you are His creation. He knows your strength and weakness as well as your fears. He knows your gifts, talents and potential. He knows what you are capable of and what you are not. If you will trust Him with your life and future, you will also be a force to reckon with. This is one if not the greatest secrets of all the men of honor the Bible talks about. You can have all the other secrets of having a successful life yet if you lack this, you are in trouble. You need the Lord to be and move with you to be able to arrive on your destined grounds. This was the difference between David and his fellows in his days. God won't send you on any mission alone nor only with just other human helpers, He will go with you. Moses knew how important this was, that was why he was unwilling to go on with the children of Israel until He had had assurance from God that He would go with them. This is also significant for us. We need God to be able to break through to our intended goal. This is our greatest strength. Anywhere men partnered with God, history was made.

Why partner with God

He can be trusted

"For I am the Lord, I changeth not; ..." Malachi 3:6

As much as we all as humans do our best towards becoming trust worthy, you cannot easily trust humans. People are not always stable. This is why you can't trust humans forever. People change but God does not. This is one of the human frailties. The Bible states that anyone who trusts in man and makes flesh his arm will be cursed. In other words put your trust in man and be disappointed. Since the beginning of the human race, history is full of stories of human disappointments and inconsistencies. Any human no matter who he or she is, might be tempted to lie, disappoint or fail his fellow human at the slightest challenge, disadvantage or discomfort. Abraham was a good man but he lied when he became afraid so as to protect himself and his family. David was the greatest King in Israel yet he cheated when he became lustful and afterwards murdered the husband of the woman he took advantage of. If you go through history you will realize that most of the troubles and wars which have occurred between people, countries, institutions and even families have resulted from some of the human inconsistencies. History is full of individuals who were once named helpful and supportive in certain institutions who later became venomous spearheading the destruction of the same institutions when they became jealous or angry. An example is Ahitophel, one of David's trusted counselors who turned against him when he was needed most. The downfall of certain empires and kingdoms has been greatly linked to treason or the betrayal of certain key individuals who were deeply involved in the affairs of those empires.

What I want you to understand is that man cannot always be trusted, and that is why you need God. He is the only one who won't leave nor forsake you. Even if you leave Him, He will still encourage you through His word waiting for a comeback. He will be with you at good times and bad times. Your secrets are secured with Him and He will never let you down no matter what happens. He will not blackmail you with your weaknesses and He will be to you an ever-present help when you need Him.

He can lead you

One of the greatest needs of men is direction. Knowing your destination is not enough to help you get there. You can't have direction without destination. But it is incomplete to also have a destination without direction. You need to know the direction to the place you intend to go. And the lack of direction is one of the reasons why people wander in life. If having a vision was all there is to achieving success, many would have been successful today. There are more you need to know after identifying what you want to achieve and one of the information you need, is knowing how to accomplish your dream. Most people know what they want but how to get it, is the issue. It is easy to have a vision but what challenges every man is how to achieve it. Life is full of men who are wandering, confused and frustrated because they are directionless. There is a scripture in

Isaiah which describes the situation of mankind; that we were all like sheep gone astray with each of us going our own ways. *"All we like sheep like sheep have gone astray; we turned every one to his own way ..."* Isaiah 53:6.

This was why mankind needed God. He is the only one who can lead you into your promised land without any mistake. He knows the end right from the beginning. He is the all-knowing God and He can help you find your way if you are lost and wandering. He knows where all the good business deals are, and can show you how to get there. He knows all the surest routes to having good success and will lead you if you allow Him. If you trust and acknowledge Him and does not lean on your own human understanding, He will direct your path. God directed the path of men who placed their trust in Him throughout scripture. And when He leads you, He will lead you beside still waters and into the paths of righteousness. *"...He leadeth me in the paths of righteousness ..."* Psalm 23:3. Your resting place will be in greener pastures and you will enjoy comfort all the way through till the accomplishment of your destiny.

He can strengthen you

Another very common need of humanity is strength and empowerment. The road to fulfillment can be very wearisome and exhausting most times due to the battles and challenges we encounter. No matter how strong you think you are, you will definitely need renewal of strength along the way. Satan knows that he cannot stop you from fulfilling your purpose in life, but can make you stop yourself if he can make you tired. This was one of the reasons why the people of Israel decided to go back to Egypt. He knows that a tired and wearied individual cannot make good decisions and choices, so he fights you by placing challenges and troubles in your path till you get tired. He knows that one of the things you will easily do when you are weary is to give up and forfeit your dream. That is why he works to make the journey more difficult for you so that you will throw down the towel. This is what happens to the people who give up in life. But the people who have God are able to sail through and accomplish their dream because he empowers them with the needed strength to carry on. He is able to strengthen you because He does not lose strength and become weary like men. The Bible says, " …that the everlasting God, the LORD, the creator of the ends of the earth, fainteth not, … He giveth power to the faint … to them that have no might he increaseth strength." Isaiah 40:28,29.

In the verse 30 of the same chapter 40, it says, ***"even the youths shall faint and be weary, and the young men shall utterly fall"***. And what the Bible means in this verse is letting you understand that no matter how strong or energetic you are, there is a possibility that you will wear out as you press on towards your goal and this is so because of the challenges on the way. But those who wait and trust in their God shall renew their strength and will soar with wings like eagles. They will run and not grow weary and will not faint if they walk. The only one who can do this is God. Men could assist you but they would get tired also and leave trying to help you but God wont. The Bible has already assured us that, He does not grow tired and weary like men. As a pastor, I have come across lots of people who have given up trying to help others because of one reason or the other. It is very rare to find men who would be willing to put their lives on the line to help others no matter what, more especially if they won't get anything in return. But the help of the Lord is sure. If you trust Him, He will be there as a source of energy and inspiration as you journey on to success.

He can protect you

According to Abraham Maslow's hierarchy of needs, security is one of the basic needs of human motivation. It is the assurance of protection from danger, damage and loss both spiritually and physically. And all humans no matter their status, rank or position in life see the feeling of safety as an essential thing to crave for especially when we live in environments that have had people's right, freedom, peace, resources, properties, life and even bodies threatened by enemies, predators, conditions and even the elements of nature. Again, another aspect which is the most important but the most commonly ignored is spiritual security and fortunately, it is going to be my emphasis in this session of the book.

We live in a physical world which is not ultimately controlled by just physical systems. There is another world beyond our physical world which is unseen but powerful and greater than this world. It is what we term spiritual realm or world and this control and influences our world all the time. Unfortunately, humanity acts and responds to things here on earth as if the spiritual does not exist. This is because our senses which enable us to access our environment cannot perceive and access the spiritual. Yet, this does not do away with the fact that it exists and that it influences our world from time to time. Science text books do not provide information on it because it can't reach it but the bible does. We are aware that there are negative forces from another side of this unseen world which is against all the good plans of God for humanity so tends to destroy the human race. Ephesians 6:12 say that, our fight is not against flesh and blood but against principality, powers, rulers of darkness, and spiritual wickedness in high places. These dark spiritual forces come to steal, kill and destroy anything good if they can. History is full of examples of men and women who were fought, victimized and destroyed by the devil. This is why you need spiritual protection more than physical protection. This is not to say physical security is unimportant. It is very good and needful but being secured spiritually is the ultimate. This is because when one is spiritually secured, the probability that he will be physically okay is high.

The reason is that the things of the spirit have the ability to influence the physical world. That is why in the book of Job, upon all that Job had, the little spiritual vulnerability could bring him disaster. You can have all forms of security physically but if you lack spiritual protection you are still in danger. One strike from the devil can wipe out everything you have toiled for, including your life. This is why we need someone who can stop and keep us from the attacks of these evil forces. And God's protection is the only surest form of security against the devil. His protection is not just to keep you from spiritual danger, damage, loss or harm but extends to the physical as well. No matter how hard you try to be secured, if you don't have God's security you are not truly secured. The Bible says that, ***"...except the Lord keeps the city, the watchman watcheth but in vain"*** (Psalm 127:1). In other words all our physical forms of security won't matter when God does not secure us. He is a strong tower and a mighty fortress. Anyone who runs to Him shall enjoy safety in all angles of life. Therefore seek God and His help and your security in life will be assured.

He can help you meet your needs

Every vision requires the right resources both material and human to make it happen. The human resource includes individuals with the knowhow and skill needed to advance your vision whereas the material resource includes every other logistics such as finance, equipment, machinery and facility. No matter how huge your dreams and aspirations are, if you lack the needed resources to keep it running, you won't be able to do much. I remember how I wasn't able to do much in my work as an evangelist who had a dream of reaching millions with the gospel of Christ all because the needed resources were not available. The business person needs a capital, just as the musician needs his instruments. I needed crusade and outreach equipment which could help me in reaching out to the masses. I know of individuals who have produced manuscripts which would change lives if they are to be published but due to unavailable financial resource those manuscripts are still unpublished. This world is full of individuals with great gifts, talents and potentials who could be outstanding and perform wonders in their respective fields should they get the needed resource to give them the push they need, but they are still in the dark because they don't have the resource and there is no one to help. This is one of the reasons why you need to first partner God before any other thing in life. He is able to give whatever you desire and expect to have so as to achieve your dream. The Bible says that, ***"…God shall supply your need aaccording to his riches in glory …"*** (Philippians 4:19). We call Him "JEHOVAH JIREH" which means "GOD OUR PROVIDER". He knows your needs and is concern about you. Unlike humans who would help you but would demand returns, He wants to help you because your happiness is His delight. He will do far more than you are expecting Him to do for you if you believe and partner Him. Remember that He is the one who created this universe and everything in it and there is nothing too hard for Him. He made Abraham wealthy when he chose to obey and walk with Him. He was the one who made sure that everything Israel needed to make their journey from Egypt to their Promised Land were provided when the need arose. And He will help you too with all that you need, including the right human resource, to make the pursuit of your dream a success when you trust Him. Seek and trust Him, and He shall meet your needs.

How to Contact and Involve God

Prayer

Prayer is one of the surest means to make contact with God and enjoy His help in all areas. It is having a communication with God. It can also be said as giving God permission to interfere in the affairs of humanity. God works where men pray. If you really want to enjoy all the benefits from having God work with you so that you can produce success, then you must learn to always be in touch with Him through prayer. It is one thing to know God but another to engage Him in your work. That is one of the best ways to enjoy good success. Wherever men had enjoyed the help of God in their lives and have been able to achieve uncommon feat in their lives, prayer had been the sure means. Wherever men prayed, uncommon things happened. Through prayer, the red sea made way for the people of Israel to pass through. We are made to understand that Elijah could do wonderful things including stopping the rain even though he was a man like everyone due to his earnestness in prayer.

Prayer always produces results and this is because prayer engages God in whatever you are doing. A friend once defined prayer as allowing God to work for and through you. Prayerful men always see results. God is everywhere, but He is not active everywhere. He is seen in action only in places where prayers are offered. David was able to achieve success in His time as a King because he was always in touch with the King of kings. He prayed three times a day and praised seven times a week according to scripture (Psalm 55:17, Psalm 119:164). One day, some Amalekites attacked the town he and his men were dwelling in their absence and took away everything including their wives and children. Whiles everyone was sorrowful complaining and blaming, he engaged God in prayer and as a result everything they lost were recovered.

Prayer has brought salvation, healing, deliverance and breakthroughs wherever men have utilized it. If you seek to excel with God, then His instruction is for you to call unto Him and He will answer. Prayer really changes things. If you get to know and understand the power in the art of prayer you will never attempt worry. That is why the Bible admonishes us in Philippians 4:6 not to worry ourselves about anything. All we are to do in order to access God's provision is to make our desire known to Him in prayers and thanksgiving.

"Be careful for nothing; but in everything by prayer and supplication with thanksgiving let youe requests be made known unto God." Philippians 4:6

Why must we pray before God Works?

If God is sovereign and can do all things, why must we pray before He does anything? If God knows all things, why must we petition before He comes to our aid? If God loves us why does He allows mankind to suffer?

These are few of the questions most Christians or pastors are asked almost every day, concerning the sovereignty of God. Why does God seem unable to do anything unless somebody prays? I thank God that we need not to worry about this, because His word answer's why things are like that.

This earth was not made for spirit beings but for human beings. According to Psalm 115:16, *the heavens are the Lord's: but the earth has He given to the children of men.* The heavens here, are the unseen world beyond this natural world. And that is where all spiritual forces inhabit. But the earth is the dwelling place for human beings and all other things whether living or non-living which can be related to with our five senses. For any being to be on earth the womb of the female is the only mode of entry or in other words the door to the earth. I believe that was why God had to use the womb as a way of entry when He wanted save mankind.

Again, spirit beings need the permission of men to be present or do anything on earth. That is the reason why whatever God wants to do on earth here, He uses human beings or better still physical beings. But even for that to work, He needs the permission of the very individuals he wants to use. That is what happened when Mary encountered angel Gabriel in the Bible concerning what God wanted to use her for. According to Luke 1:38, right after she said for it to be done in her life just as the angel had said, he departed. God needs you to permit Him to work for you. And one way to do that is to pray. Prayer engages God in things concerning humanity. In Ezekiel 36 God spoke through the prophet about things He wanted to do for His children. He gave them very wonderful promises but then in the verse 37 of the same chapter He tells them to come and ask Him to do the very same things He promised to do for them. *"Thus saith the Lord GOD; I will yet for this be enquired of by the house of Israel, to do it for them ...*" Ezekiel 36:37. I remember how I once use to wonder why things we were like this until I stumbled upon other scriptures. John Wesley said, "God does nothing except in response to believing prayer."

But again, one of the reasons why it seems like evil or bad things easily happen on this earth is that the devil was legally allowed here by Adam. We know of how after God created the heaven and the earth and then furnished everything in it, He handed over everything in it to Adam, the first man He made. In Genesis 1:28, the Bible says, " *...and God said unto them, Be fruitful, and multiply, and replenish the earth, and subdue it; and then have dominion over the fish of the sea, and over the fowl of the air, and over every living thing that moveth upon the earth*". Man became the landlord of the earth until he traded his position to the devil. In Luke 4:5,6, the devil made Jesus aware of his position as the in charge of the world and its kingdoms since it was delivered unto him. By his position as the god of this earth, he is able to do most of the things he uses people to do on earth. But thank God that through Jesus Christ, man was restored.

May be you are surprised about how negative things seem to be happening to this world or your life and how it seems that God does not care. I want you to understand that God cares and would want to help you achieve your dream if only you will engage Him in prayer. He is waiting for you to call on Him. Stop complaining about the things you do not like and start establishing what you desire through prayers. Mark 11:24 says, "*whatsoever things you desire when you pray, believe that you have received them and you will have them*". The emphasis is on "whatsoever things you desire, when you pray". This means that desires are establish in prayers. Do you have any desire, please get up and pray and you will see them. Jesus, in teaching His disciples on prayer said to them to always pray that the will of God will be done on earth the way it is documented in heaven. Which meant that what might be happening to you on earth could be contrary to the will God. One thing I realized in life is that bad things happen without any difficulty but we require effort to enforce good things to happen. To constantly witness the will of God in your life as a good partner of God, you need to get yourself committed to continuous prayer. That is why we are advised in the Bible to pray without ceasing.

Praying is also communing or fellowshipping with God. How can you even have a fruitful partnership with someone you don't often talk to or someone you don't get involve with? To have a fruitful partnership with someone there are very common things you will need to have. They include having common interest, vision, and belief about what you intend to achieve together. And it is through prayer that you are able to internalize, assimilate, understand and agree to the ideas, principles and plans God has for you. By praying we get to know what He wants us to do and also receive inspiration, direction and leading since He knows best and can take us through the right path which leads to our destiny.

In his book, "The message that works", Dr. T. L. Osborn defines prayer as harmonizing our spirits and emotions with the Holy Spirits until His plan becomes our consuming passion. Through prayers, we are able to conceive God inspired ideas and concepts for the achievements of our dream. Lastly it is through prayer that we are able to tap into divine strength and ability to do extra ordinary things. In Acts 4, the Bible records that the disciples of Jesus one day met to pray when their work was challenged and threatened, and when they had done that, they were all filled with the Holy Ghost, and they spake the Word of God in boldness. The verse 33 of the chapter says, **"and with great power gave the apostles a witness of the resurrection of the Lord Jesus: and great grace was upon them all."**

Faith in His Word

The second surest way to contact God is by knowing and practicing His Word. This might seem a little strange to those who are not

Christians but not to Christians. We don't only believe that there is a God, but also believe that He has given mankind His Word, which is the Bible. The Bible does not just reveal God but reveal His intent, ideals and principles for making the universe and everything in it. Before we were informed about universal laws whether the law of physics, law of chemistry, the law of biogenesis, the law of mathematics or the law of logic through which this universe works by science, the Bible had already mentioned it, though it does not give any detailed information. Jeremiah 33:26 calls it the *"ordinances of heaven and earth"*.

What the Bible is very precise and detailed on are moral laws which are also universal in themselves. Just as the laws of nature are given to ensure harmony and order in the universe, moral laws are also given to ensure that humans enjoy life just as God planned it to be on earth. We know that without the law of gravity lives couldn't have existed on this planet, due to the fact that it is that law which holds things together. The same way, without the moral laws given by God in His Word, or even by their disregard we would destroy ourselves on this earth. I hope with this you can understand why things are in a mess on the earth right now.

Many have asked where all those life destructive hazards humanity is faced with right now are from and why we are plagued with them. Some blame it on the God of the universe whereas others blame other things. But the truth is that human activities or actions stemming from human nature like selfishness, greed, and ignorance have led to the woes we see. God is not the one destroying this world or human lives, we are. It is true that God gave human beings the free will to do things and choose how we will live, but then He shows us by His Word how life works and how things should be, here on earth, though He does not force us. I believe this is so that we would not blame Him for the bad things that happen.

No one knows life best than its giver who is God, and He is the best person to tell us how it works. That was why Jesus came. He came to show us the way of life. In John 10: 10, He clearly shows us that He came to give us abundance of life. If you want to know how life works, get into the Bible. Just as God's greatest gift to the Jews is His commandments, laws and precepts, His greatest gift to all mankind is His Word revealed by Jesus and remember that Jesus didn't destroy the Jewish laws but fulfilled them. God's idea is not religion but showing the human race the best way they can live and enjoy the life He gave them. That is the reason for His Word. His Word is His standard for human life on earth, nothing below it or above it.

Embracing the words of Jesus is embracing the best way of life whereas rejecting it is programming your way to self-destruction or doom. Many people think that Christianity frightens or scare the hell out of people with doom or hell fire. That is not what the gospel message says. The gospel of Christ is God's song of salvation from self-destruction. You will realize that almost all those acts called sins recorded in scripture are the actions of men that bring destruction to themselves. Like I said before, God is not the one destroying the human race, humanity is destroying itself. Today, science reports on how humanity is fast approaching self-destruction.

Top scientists like Professor Frank Fenner and Stephen Hawking predicts that humanity has less than 100 years to act so as to save the race due to certain activities of humanity that is destroying the earth. God is a life giver, not a destroyer. He is not destroying anyone; all He wants us to do is to choose the more excellent way of life demonstrated in Christ Jesus. And this is what the Word of God talks about. The good news of Christ is God's message of mercy, kindness and love towards the human race. God's Word shows us how to live effectively and enjoy life. It also shows us how to stay away from doom. The Bible is full of the stories of how men who embraced God's Word prospered and enjoyed life, and also the end of those who rejected His Word. Deuteronomy 28: 1 assures any nation who shall set themselves to do and follow God's commands that they will be high above every nations of the earth. It again says in the verse 13 of the same chapter 28 of Deutronomy that, *"the LORD shall make thee the head, and not the tail; and thou shalt be above only, and thou shalt not be beneath; if that thou hearken unto the commandments of the LORD thy God."*

Understand that embracing the Word of God will distinguish you from those who reject it. Get to know the mind of your creator by giving yourself to the study and practice of His Word. Build your life on the solid Word of God and you will go far. Church history shows that ministries which are able to stand the test of time and endure the storms of life are those founded on the teaching of the solid Word of God. The Bible says that, those who build their life on the word are like a man who builds his house on a rock. Such a house will never collapse or come down when the storms of life come because of the foundation on which it is built. But the other who had his house collapsing when the storms came is the one who built his house on sand. And this signifies that that man didn't build his life on the solid Word of God, hence the destruction that came to him. Embrace the Word of God and you will make wonderful strides in life.

What the Word Will Do For You

It helps in self-discovery

Just as a manufacturer's manual helps any individual to get the most out of any machine or equipment, the Word of God too is God's manual which helps individuals to make discoveries of who they are and what they are made to do. James 1:23-24, says, *"For if any be hearer of the word, and not a doer, he is like unto a man beholding his natural face in a glass: for he beholdeth himself, and goeth his way, and straightway forgetteth what manner of man he was."*

This implies that we see ourselves when we study God's Word. God is your creator and it is He alone who knows what you are made up of. So by going deeper in His word you discover who you are, what you have and what you can do. It will help you to understand why you exist and how you can live to fulfill that. Let me repeat this; no one is useless in life. Every one of us was created for a reason. And through the Word of God you will get to understand your place and position on earth.

It helps in character development and modification

God's Word is the most astounding book on character development which you can find anywhere. You will realize that the New Testament is full of messages on building the right character and habits for effective living. Galatians 5:22-23 give a list of very important virtues which can ensure fruitful living on earth. These include virtues like love, joy, peace, patience, kindness, goodness, faithfulness, humility, and self-control. It is the book which deals with all the basic characteristic of human nature which includes selfishness, greed and ignorance. It is one of the best books that encourage education.

It makes us aware of what ignorance can do to us (Read Hosea 4:6, Isaiah 5:13) and how it can be solved (Read 2 Timothy 2:15). It also highlights more on selflessness as one of the core ways to live. It teaches about giving one's self to helping others. And again, it shows how one can be content, yet press on to do more.

It Unveils God's will to us

One of the effective ways to be successful in your walk or partnership with God is to know and do His will. We have already learnt that to be able to excel and make unforgettable impression in life and in this world, we cannot take God out of our lives. Therefore we need to know how to partner and engage the hand of God in what we do. But then, for an effective partnership with Him, we need to cooperate with Him on His intent, concept and will for us. That is the only way you can live to please Him. Knowing what

His expectations are for you and what He wants you to accomplish here on earth is very important for a successful walk. For effective cooperation in your partnership with God, you need to be able know what He wants from you. The Bible explains that, two people cannot have a fruitful walk together unless they agree (Read Amos 3:3). And how can you walk in agreement with a partner when you do not know his or her intent. Similarly, your walk with God cannot be fruitful when you don't have any idea of what pleases Him. And so to be able to have a fair knowledge of His will for every individual on earth, He gave us His Word so that we will be able to know what His plans are for each of us.

It will heal you

God's word is a great medicine to all the wounds of humanity, if only we will give it the attention needed. King Solomon was advised in Proverbs 4:22 by his father to not let the Word depart from him, for it is life to those who find them, and also health to their flesh. Proverbs 3:8 says that *"it shall be health to thy navel, and marrow to thy bones."* According to Psalm 107:20, God *sent his word, and healed them, and delivered them from their destructions.* We are grateful to God for the great breakthrough the field of medicine has achieved so far in the twenty first century, yet we cannot compare the results of medical science to the great part the word of God can play if mankind will begin to access its truths and revelations.

The Word of God does not just help in addressing physical sickness and diseases of mankind, but also the areas that that physical science cannot reach. It brings healing to both the spirit and the soul of a man. To the Word, there is nothing like incurable diseases if only we will utilize its power. In Roman 1:16 we learn that it is the power of God to bring salvation to them who believe it. We know that, the most powerful gift given to humanity by God is His Word. Spiritually, it brings redemption and transformation to the human spirit. When we believe and accept His word on the salvation of humanity we become recreated beings in our spirit. We become liberated from our formal sinful nature and take up a new, glorious and lively nature.

Psychologically, the Word of God brings peace of mind to those who believe and accepts it. It delivers us from the three main psychological problem of man, which are fear, guilt and anger. The Bible clearly states that, it is the knowledge of the truth (Word) which leads to freedom. Again, it is one of the greatest books given to show mankind how to recover from the mistakes, defeats and failure we encounter when we go against the laws which binds life.

Believe God's Word and you won't be disappointed. If you don't have any knowledge about what God is saying about life, you and the world, then get a Bible and give yourself to its wisdom and you will never regret. There are lots of truths and revelations you need to discover about God and yourself. Become a student and doer of His Word and you will never be ashamed.

Conclusion

In closing, I want you to understand these three things,

The first thing I would want you to know is that you are special no matter your race, tribe, tongue or background. You are one of God's creative master piece. You are not ordinary. There is nobody ever like you on this planet. You are a great blessing so do not despise yourself. You are not useless no matter your status or level in life. God made you for a purpose on this earth, and it is mainly to solve an existing problem. This is your destiny. You are an asset so don't make yourself a liability.

The second thing is that God loves you so much that He wants you to have the best of life even when it required Him to allow His Son come and fulfill all the conditions for your happiness and peace in life. Your destiny is revealed when you encounter the living Christ Jesus.

And lastly this world is waiting for your manifestation. Do not be limited by your situation or condition. Understand that all that you require to impact this world is already within you. And that nothing can stop you if you make up your mind to rise and influence the world for God. This is the reason for this book. I ask that by this book, you will encounter a turnaround in your life. Stay blessed!

References

1. Unless otherwise indicated, all Scripture quotations are taken from the New King James Version, ©1979,1980,1982 by Thomas Nelson, Inc.

2. Hill N. (2000) *"The Law of Success."* Wilshire Book Company, ISBN: 0879804475, 9780879804473

3. Murdock M. (2002) *"The Assignment."* Thomas Nelson Incorporated. ISBN: 0785265171, 9780785265177.

4. Hubpages (2014) Importance of planning Retreived from: [http://hubpages.com/business/The-Importance-of-Planning]

5. www.brainyquote.com (2001-2016) *"All quotes".* Retrieved from; [https://www.brainyquote.com/]

Printed in the United States
By Bookmasters